Forex Investing for Beginners, Dummies & Idiots

By Giovanni Rigters

© Copyright 2021 - All rights reserved.

The contents of this book may not be reproduced, duplicated or transmitted without direct written permission from the author.

Under no circumstances will any legal responsibility or blame be held against the publisher for any reparation, damages, or monetary loss due to the information herein, either directly or indirectly.

Legal Notice:

This book is copyright protected. This is only for personal use. You cannot amend, distribute, sell, use, quote or paraphrase any part or the content within this book without the consent of the author.

Disclaimer Notice:

Please note the information contained within this document is for educational and entertainment purposes only. Every attempt has been made to provide accurate, up to date and reliable complete information. No warranties of any kind are expressed or implied. Readers acknowledge that the author is not engaging in the rendering of legal, financial, medical or professional advice. The content of this book has been derived from various sources. Please consult a licensed professional before attempting any techniques outlined in this book.

By reading this document, the reader agrees that under no circumstances is the author responsible for any losses, direct or indirect, which are incurred as a result of the use of information contained within this document, including, but not limited to, — errors, omissions, or inaccuracies.

Risk Disclaimer

Please note that trading the Forex exchange market on margin is highly risky and may not be a good fit for all investors. Before you decide to trade Forex, think carefully about your investment goals, experience level, and risk appetite. There is a possibility that you can sustain losses of some of your capital or all your capital, so do not invest money you can't afford to lose. Be aware of the attendant risks of Forex trading, and get advice from an independent, accredited advisor if you have any questions or doubts.

All news, opinion, research, prices, analyses, and other information contained in this book are provided only as general market commentary, do not constitute investment or trading advice, and should not be considered as such. The author will not accept liability for any loss or damage, including and without limitation to any loss of profit, which may arise directly or indirectly from the use of or reliance on the information in this book.

The contents of this book are subject to change at any time with no prior notice and are given for the sole and express purpose of helping traders make their independent trading and investing decisions.

The author has taken all due measures to ensure the information in this book is accurate. However, this doesn't guarantee its accuracy. Therefore, the author will not accept liability for any damage or loss that may come from directly or indirectly applying the information in this book or the reader's inability to understand the information herein correctly.

Table of Contents

Introduction

Chapter One: An Intro to Forex Trading
Forex Trading Sessions
Currencies
Crosses and Minors
Other Crosses
The Exotics
Volume
How You Make Money Trading Forex
Base and Quote Currencies

Chapter Two: Your Forex Account
The Spread: Bid and Ask Prices
All About Pips
Types of Orders
Placing Trades

Chapter Three: Analyzing the Markets and Yourself
Fundamental Analysis
Trading Fundamentals
What Kind of Trader Are You?

Chapter Four: Lines, Bars, Candlesticks
Candlestick Patterns
Chart Patterns

 Symmetrical Triangles
 Flags and Pennants
 Wedges
 Rectangles
 A Final Note on Trading Patterns

Chapter Five: Technical Trading Strategies
 Let's Talk Trends
 More on Support and Resistance
 Support and Resistance: Market Maker Style
 Pivot Points
 Pivot Points in Day Trading
 Pivots for Entries and Exits

Chapter Six: Moving Averages
 The Simple Moving Average
 The Exponential Moving Average
 Trading MA Crossovers
 Ribbon Trading

Chapter Seven: Spotting Trade Setups
 Your Trading Routine
 Multi Time Frame Analysis
 The Importance of Trend Lines
 The Lows and Highs of Trading
 Fibonacci Retracements
 Momentum, Timing, Entries, and Exits
 Using Candlestick Formations

Chapter Eight: Managing the Trade

Tweaking Your Trade Plan with Time

Chapter Nine: Risk, Money, and Emotional Management

Risk Reward Ratios

Money Management

Chapter Ten: Mistakes Forex Traders Make

Conclusion

References

Introduction

Forex trading is a great way to make some money, whether as a side income or a full-time job. However, there are so many things you need to work out when it comes to trading that it can feel very overwhelming.

There is a mind-boggling amount of information on the Internet about how to trade Forex, to the point where it's become difficult to sift through the nonsense and find real gold you can use to take your trading skills to a pro-level. So, where do you begin? Also, with the number of fake traders and scammers out there, who do you trust? Everyone wants to sell you their course, their signals, their books. So, which ones are worth spending money on?

I've written this book for you, dear would-be trader, because, like you, I once struggled with all of this. Whether you're just starting out, or you've been at this long enough to wish you hadn't even discovered Forex trading, I feel your pain. I have been scammed a few times by fake mentors and gurus, spent lots of money on fancy EAs and indicators that were a whole lot of nothing, and believed a lie about what to expect from trading Forex.

Thankfully, I found my way out of all that mess, and now I want nothing more than to pass on to you everything I have learned along my journey that has helped me become consistently profitable.

This book is nothing like all the others out there, as you will read. Instead, it comes straight from the heart and cuts right down to the stuff that actually matters, the things you need to know that will help you grow from a neophyte trader to a pro in your own right. In this book, I will tell you the truth about Forex trading and the mindset you need to succeed. There will be no sugar coating because it's all that sugar that leads to many new traders' frustrations.

By the end of this book, you will most likely discover that you've always been a good trader, but you just weren't given one or more of the primary keys to the kingdom of blue pips. Or, if you're a complete newbie, you will thank the stars that this was the book you chose out of all the others out there.

The entire Forex industry feels like a big, strange world, but you don't have to worry about getting lost in it. Instead, I'll hold your hand through every page of this book and show you what you need to know and do to turn the corner and become consistently profitable. The information in this book isn't the Holy Grail, but it will prove instrumental to your success.

Chapter One: An Intro to Forex Trading

Forex is short for "foreign exchange." It is a worldwide financial market that allows the banks - and you - to trade currencies. The concept behind trading the market is simple speculation. If you're confident one currency will go up against the other, you buy it, and then you can make a profit.

Here's an illustration: When traveling to other countries, chances are you've had to swap your dollars or whatever currency you use in your country for the currency of trade in your destination country. There, you may have noticed that there's a screen that shows you different currency rates. These are called exchange rates, and they represent the price of one currency relative to another.

Exchange rates let you know how many Swiss Francs you'll get in exchange for the twenty-dollar bill in your hand. When you make the exchange, what you've essentially done is sold US dollars for Swiss Francs, or in Forex parlance, you went "short on USD/CHF."

When you're heading back to the states, then you've got to swap your Francs for US dollars again, or "go long on USD/CHF." When you're trading Forex, you want to make a profit from determining which one of two currencies will be weaker than the other and then choosing to buy strength and sell weakness. That's it.

Also called the FX market, the foreign exchange market is the world's largest, decentralized, global market that allows currencies to be exchanged. While the prices of each currency may seem relatively stable at the bureau de change where you swapped dollars for francs, the exchange rates change from second to second.

This market boasts $6.6 trillion in the volume of trading transactions each day. The bulk of those transactions are carried by central banks, large banks, hedge funds, and other financial institutions. These markets stay open for retail traders (that's you and me) 24 hours a day, 6 days a week (Sunday to Friday). They stay open for the "big boys" (the bankers) during the weekends, though, which is why you see gaps in the market price when you open up your charts by the next trading week.

Forex Trading Sessions

There are three main trading sessions in the Forex market where you can get ample liquidity to trade. They are the **Asian, London,** and **New York** sessions, with the last two being more liquid than the first one. On account of Daylight Savings, the times may vary.

So, to know which session you're trading, depending on where you are in the world, check out Forexmartkethours.com. It's a great free website that allows you to put in your time zone and see where each session begins and ends for you in your corner of the world.

You really only want to trade during London and New York. It's not that trading Asia is impossible. It's just that the other two markets give ample movement for you to squeeze some pips out. So if you really want a market that moves, check out the London/New York overlap when both markets are active.

While bond and stock markets close at the end of the business day, the Forex market stays "awake," simply moving to another financial center in the world. A typical trading day begins with the Asian session before moving on to the London session and then the New York session.

Currencies

In Forex, you trade currencies. You're not buying the physical Yen or Euro, but you're speculating on their values. It's almost like buying a share in the economy of various countries (or selling one).

Major currencies are the ones that are traded the most because they are made up of the largest economies in the world. They are:

- USD: The United States Dollar, also called the Buck.
- EUR: The Eurozone Euro, also called the Fiber.
- JPY: The Japanese Yen

- GBP: The Great British Pound, also called the Cable.
- CHF: The Switzerland Franc, also called the Swissy.
- CAD: The Canadian Dollar, also called the Loonie
- AUD: The Australian Dollar, called the Aussie
- NZD: The New Zealand Dollar, called the Kiwi

You've probably noticed that they all have three letters called the ISO 4217 Currency Codes, established by the International Organization for Standardization (ISO) in 1973. The first two letters are made up of the country's name, while the last one is the currency's name.

You trade currencies through a broker, and they are always traded in pairs. This is because each one is quoted relative to another. For instance, you have the popular Euro against the US dollar, called EUR/USD. Then there's the Swissy against the Yen, which is CHF/JPY. So, you can only ever trade Forex in pairs, buying or selling one for the other.

There are three kinds of currency pairs:

- The majors, which always have the US dollar as one side of the equation.
- The crosses, which do not have the US dollar, ever (also called minors).

- The exotics, which have one major currency paired against an emerging economy's currency.

In Forex, the price of the majors moves a lot more than the exotics and the crosses, as they are the most traded pairs. This means you'll get a lot of trading opportunities with them. They are:

- EUR/USD (Euro Dollar)
- USD/JPY (Dollar Yen)
- GBP/USD (Pound Dollar)
- USD/CHF (Dollar Swissy)
- USD/CAD (Dollar Loonie)
- AUD/USD (Aussie Dollar)
- NZD/USD (Kiwi Dollar)

The majors are the most liquid pairs you can trade. When I say "liquid," I mean that they have a lot of financial activity. So, the next time you hear the word "liquidity," you'll know what that means. A market is liquid because of the volume of trading activity.

Crosses and Minors

Crosses are pairs that don't have the USD in them. They aren't often traded like the minors, but they are relatively liquid, so they can still give you generous trading opportunities. The most-traded crosses are pairs that have EUR, JPY, and GBP.

Euro Crosses

- EUR/CHF or the Euro Swissy
- EUR/CAD or the Euro Loonie
- EUR/GBP or the Euro Pound
- EUR/NZD or the Euro Kiwi
- EUR/AUD or the Euro Aussie
- EUR/SEK or the Euro Stockie
- EUR/NOK or the Euro Nockie

Yen Crosses

- EUR/JPY or the Euro Yen
- GBP/JPY or the Pound Yen (Also called the "guppy" or "the dragon")
- CAD/JPY or the Loonie Yen
- CHF/JPY or the Swissy Yen
- AUD/JPY or the Aussie Yen
- NZD/JPY or the Kiwi Yen

Pound Crosses

- GBP/CAD or the Pound Loonie
- GBP/AUD or the Pound Aussie
- GBP/CHF or the Pound Swissy
- GBP/NZD or the Pound Kiwi

Other Crosses

- AUD/CAD or the Aussie Loonie (Or Aussie CAD)
- AUD/CHF or the Aussie Swissy
- AUD/NZD or the Aussie Kiwi

- CAD/CHF or the Loonie Swissy (Or CAD Swiss)
- NZD/CAD or the Kiwi Loonie (Or Kiwi CAD)
- NZD/CHF or the Kiwi Swissy

The Exotics

These pairs have one primary currency pegged to the currency of EM's or emerging economies like Mexico, Brazil, Hungary, Turkey, or Chile. Not every broker offers these pairs to trade, but here's a list of the currencies you may find on yours, paired against the US dollar, Euro, and Pound:

- The Brazilian Real (BRL)
- The Hong Kong Dollar (HKD)
- The Saudi Arabian Riyal (SAR)
- The Singaporean Dollar (SGD)
- The South African Rand (ZAR)
- The Thailand Baht (THB)
- The Russian Ruble (RUB)
- The Mexican Peso (MXN)
- The Polish Zloty (PLN)
- The Chilean Peso (CLP)
- The Norwegian Krone (NOK)
- The Swedish Krona (SEK)

There are several other exotic currencies you could trade, but these are the most commonly offered ones. With the exotics, you will find that the spreads are several times larger than with the majors. This is because they don't have as much liquidity, and they're usually a lot more affected by economic events and geopolitical news. For example, if a war breaks out in one of these countries, potentially causing the price of that currency to drastically plummet relative to the major currencies, creating more movement than you could ever find on the majors. This is something to keep in mind if you choose to trade these pairs.

Volume

Volume is the amount of the currency pair being traded over time. It's about the number of units that are exchanged between buyers and sellers. There are certain times when the markets aren't quite as liquid as you'd like them to be. In these times, the volumes of trades are too low to make anything out of it - unless your trading strategy requires that you have low volume and liquidity to begin with.

Volume is essential because you need it to confirm that the patterns you see on your charts are actually valid and that the market is really moving in the direction you think it is. When there are significant changes in the asset price with high volume, that means the move is more important, and you should look for ways to get in on that. So, volume is beneficial when you're analyzing price movement.

Trade Anywhere, Anytime

The Forex market isn't like the London Stock Exchange or the New York Stock Exchange, where all trading happens in one location. Instead, this is an over-the-counter market, which means it's all done electronically, on the interbank network, 24 hours a day, and for retail traders, six days a week. As long as you have an Internet connection, then you can trade.

While you can trade whenever you want to, a good rule of thumb is to avoid trading on Sundays, Mondays, and Fridays. On the first two days, the market needs time to determine how to respond to weekend news, and you should also allow it to show you where it wants to go.

On Fridays, the volume can be low (or there may be too much volatility on account of significant news releases). Bank holidays are an excellent time to stay out unless you have experience trading at these times and a broker who gives you a fair spread. Finally, do not trade significant news events.

You can tell when they're about to happen by going to Forex Factory's website and checking the news calendar. Anything flagged as high or medium means you should stay out until at least five minutes after the news release.

Getting A Broker

When you want to find a broker, you want one with tight spreads. The tighter the spreads, the faster you can get into profit on your trades, and the quicker you can make them risk-free by moving your stop loss to break even.

Also, you want a broker who has accreditation from the national regulatory bodies so that they will treat you fairly and so that you're protected if you and your broker have a dispute that wasn't your fault, to begin with, and costs you money.

Be sure to get familiar with their terms and conditions before you sign up for an account. This way, you already know what you're getting into. For example, some brokers don't allow hedging (trading in both directions) or scalping (entering trades with colossal lot sizes only to get out in a matter of minutes or seconds with a few pips of profit). So, you want to know what's good and what may lead to a termination of your account.

Most brokers offer demo accounts, so you can paper trade or demo trade and get a feel for what trading is like. Now, you should keep in mind that demo trading isn't the same as live trading, psychologically or financially. The demo trading lets you get used to the trading platform, practice your strategy to see how viable it is, and test other parameters with your trading.

You cannot withdraw demo money. If you could, we'd all be retired. Also, you'll find that you might get excellent fills on price when trading the news with a demo account, but this is not guaranteed when you're in the live markets with real funds. This is just something to keep in mind if you stubbornly decide to trade the news.

Check out the reviews for the brokers before you choose one. You can look them up on Forex Peace Army. You want a broker with good reviews but be careful that they aren't paid reviews. You'll know it's fake when they all sound generic or come on the same day or from the same place. Also, a good broker will usually respond to any negative complaints or issues on this forum, intending to clear the air or fix any problems. If they're still replying even now, chances are they are a broker you can trust.

Good brokers also offer you various trading platforms, from the tried-and-true Metatrader 4 to Metatrader 5 (Android, Apple, Web, and Desktop versions are usually given) to the sleek and modern cTrader (also available for phone, desktop, and Web).

There are two kinds of brokers: the **market makers** and the **Electronic Communications Networks (ECN).** The former set their own prices with the ask and spread and manipulate prices to take out stop losses. The latter use the best ask and bid prices they can get from interbank institutions and usually charge a tiny commission for your trades. It's up to you to work out which kind you prefer.

Beware that some brokers go rogue, manipulating their prices to rip off traders, slowing down execution time for your trades, refusing to honor your stop loss and take profit levels, and more. So, you really should take your time when choosing one. I won't recommend a broker in this book, but if you do your homework and follow the criteria given here, you'll find a great broker to trade with.

How You Make Money Trading Forex

You make money by selling or buying currencies. In Forex-speak, "going **long** on the Euro Dollar" means you're going to buy the Euro, expecting that it will rise in value relative to the Dollar. "Going **short** on the Euro Dollar" means you expect that the Euro's value will fall relative to the Dollar, and so you will sell.

You may also hear the terms **bullish** and **bearish**. Buyers are the bulls in the market, pushing prices higher, while sellers are the bears. When you have no positions running, that means you're **square** or **flat**.

The point of trading is to make money from the price difference. If you're bullish on the Dollar versus the Loonie, that means you expect to make money as the price goes higher from when you placed your trade. When you're bearish, you hope to make money as the exchange price between those currencies goes lower, in your favor.

In a bullish scenario, you could buy 10,000 Great British Pounds against the Dollar at the exchange rate of 1.17000.

GBP 10,000 x 1.17 = US $11,700

Then a couple of weeks later, the price rallies to 1.2500. So, you liquidate or close that trade.

GBP 10,000 x 1.25 = US $12,500.

In this case, you've made $800 in profit.

The exchange rate between both currencies in GBP/CAD shows you how many pounds you can buy with one Canadian Dollar or how many loonies you need to buy one pound.

Base and Quote Currencies

To trade successfully, you need to know how to read the Forex quotes. As mentioned before, they always are written in pairs. The first currency in a pair is the base currency. For example, the base currency in EUR/NOK is the Euro. It is the reference currency and is always worth just 1. The second currency is the quote currency (also called the counter currency). In our example, that would be the Norwegian Krona.

So, the exchange rate lets you know how many units of the quote currency you will need before you can buy 1 unit of the base currency. So, if the price of EUR/USD is 1.77351, that means you need to pay 1.77351 US Dollars to buy 1 Euro. When you're selling, the exchange rate will let you know how many units of the counter currency you will get for selling 1 unit of the base currency. This means you will get 1.77351 when you sell 1 Euro.

There is a standard for quoting Forex currency pairs that all brokers respect, so you never have to worry about which one is the base or the quote. Just know that EUR/USD will always be EUR/USD, not USD/EUR. There may be a slash, a dot, or nothing at all in between the currencies listed on your broker. In the end, it's all the same.

Chapter Two: Your Forex Account

The Spread: Bid and Ask Prices

Forex quotes always have two prices called the bid and the ask. The bid is the price your broker offers to exchange the base currency for the quote. It's the price the broker buys from you when you sell. So, to keep this simple, anytime you sell a pair, you will be offered the bid price.

The ask is the price at which you exchange the quoted currency for the base. In other words, it's the price you get to buy the currency pair at if you choose to get into a trade.

The spread is the difference between the asking price and the bidding price. So, if you put a trade on, you will always pay the spread.

When you want to sell GBP/USD, all you do is click the sell button, and you will be offered the bid price, which shows up as a line on your chart. When you buy GBP/USD, you'll get the asking price. The bid price is always lower than the asking price. It makes sense because if you're going to make a profit, you should buy low and sell high.

You want to make a profit, and so does your broker. One of the ways they make their money is through the spread. That's why when you put a trade on, you're immediately a few pips or pipettes (or points) in the red. Your broker may also charge you a commission for each transaction, especially if they offer really tight spreads.

All About Pips

Trading is about making pips and keeping them. A pip is the measurement of the change in value between currencies, and it is made up of ten points or pipettes (but nobody really talks about points or pipettes all that much in Forex).

When GBP/USD moves from 1.35500 to 1.35510, it has moved by one pip, which is 0.0001. A quick note: Some brokers are five-digit brokers, which means the number of figures after a decimal point is always five, except for Yen pairs, where the digits after the decimal are always three. These are fractional pips, and they are always a tenth of a full pip. So, say price moved from 1.35500 to 1.35513, that means price moved by 13 points or pipettes, or by 1.3 pips.

Other brokers are four-digit brokers, which means they only use four digits after a decimal point, and two digits on Yen pairs. So, in our example, the price moved by 1 pip, not 10 pips. Many newbies make the rookie mistake of saying they made a hundred pips when they really made 10.

To give another illustration, when the price moves from 119.200 to 119.210 on USD/JPY, it has moved by just one pip. If it moved to 119.213, then it moved by 1.3 pips or 13 points.

Calculating Pip Values

Every currency has its own value relative to others, which means every currency pair pays out different amounts. To keep things simple, I'll revert to using just four digits when quoting prices so that you can work out the math quickly.

Assume that USD/CHF is at 1.0400. This means 1 USD equals 1.04 CHF. To calculate the value change of just 1 pip, you divide that pip by the exchange rate value and multiply it by one.

1 Pip = 0.0001 CHF

Exchange ratio = 1 USD/1.0400 CHF

[0.0001/1.0400] x 1 = 0.00009615 USD per unit, approximately. So, if you trade 10,000 units of USD/CHF, then when the price changes by a pip, that would be a change of USD 0.96 approximately.

Your trading account could be in a different currency other than the dollar. This means you need to work out the value of a pip differently. Just divide or multiply the pip value you arrive at using the method above by your account currency's exchange rate position.

If this all seems a bit too much for you, don't sweat it. Your broker already automatically works it out for you, and you could always go online to use free pip value calculators.

Lots

The amounts you trade in are known as lots. These are the number of units of each currency sold or bought. Lots are how you measure the size of your trade transaction. Every time you put an order on, it's quoted in lots.

- **The standard lot size** has 100,000 currency units.
- **The mini lot size** has 10,000 currency units
- **Micro lots** have 1,000 currency units
- **Nano lots** (rarely used) have 100 currency units

Some brokers forego lots and show you the value of your trade-in currency units, but lots are really a lot more convenient. For you to take advantage of the movement in price or pips, you need to have access to large amounts of a currency before you can gain actual profits (or make significant losses, because that happens too.)

If you're using a standard lot, let's see how that will change the value of a pip for you:

If USD/JPY is at an exchange rate of 118.90: (0.02/118.90) x 100,000 = GBP 8.4 x 118.90

If USD/CAD is at an exchange rate of 1.5000: (0.0002/1.5000) x 100,000 = $6.9 per pip.

When the base currency isn't the dollar, the math changes:

If GBP/USD is at an exchange rate of 1.1830: (0.0001/1.1830) x 100,000 = 8.5 x 1.1830 = $10 per pip, approximately. Your broker will let you know the value of each pip on their website, or you can just send them an inquiry.

Leverage

The money you trade as part of retail is nothing compared to what the Central Banks trade. You can't make any money with it unless your broker gives you leverage. The leverage available to you depends on your broker and your risk appetite.

First, you must make a deposit with your broker. This is known as **margin**. Then your broker will let you know how much of that margin you need to trade your positions.

Say your leverage is 100:1, which is 1 percent of the position in question, and you want to trade a position that's worth $100,000. But then, the trouble is all you have is $10,000 as your margin. Your broker will then parcel off $1,000 of your margin for the trade and allow you to borrow the remaining $99,000. If you make any profits, they show up in your account balance and increase your margin.

If you lose, your account balance goes down. The minimum margin requirement differs from one broker to the next. So, with a broker who asks for a 1 percent margin, each $100,000 position you trade will require a deposit of $1,000.

Please know that the margin requirement isn't a fee but a deposit. In other words, it will still be there after you've closed your trade (assuming you closed in profit). If you're in a trade and your account balance goes below $1,000, then you get a margin call, which is when the broker stops you out of your trade. If they don't do this, there's a risk of your account going into the negative, and then you'll owe them money.

Types of Orders

An order tells your broker to open or close a trade on your behalf if it meets the requirements you set for them. There are two basic kinds of orders: **Market orders** and **pending orders.**

The market order is executed right away, with the current price that your broker is offering you. You use a pending order when you'd rather execute your trade at a different price than what the broker's offering currently.

There are various kinds of pending orders. If you want to buy at a lower price than the current price, you place a **buy limit order.** If you want to buy at a higher price than you have on your chart at the moment, you set a **buy stop order.** If you're going to sell higher than the spot price, you place a **sell limit order.** Want to sell lower? Then set a **sell stop**

order. These orders remain pending, only to be executed if the price arrives at your specified level.

You also have a stop-loss order. This is very important, and if you know how to use it correctly with a good strategy, it will save you from going bust when you have losing trades. For example, say you want to buy at 1.5010. You'd put your stop loss ten pips away, which is 1.5000. If the price moves down against your position, once it hits the 1.5010, your broker will close the trade to protect you from losing any more money.

There's the **take profit order,** which tells your broker when to take you out of a successful trade. Once you're in a trade, and you were right about the direction, your broker will close it for you at that level so that you can keep the pips you made. There's no point in trading if you're going to keep leaving money on the table.

When you're trading, you don't have to exit a trade completely if you don't want to. Instead, you could choose to protect the profits you make with a different kind of stop-loss order, called the **trailing stop.** The trailing stop adjusts itself along with the fluctuations of price. For instance, say you have a stop loss of 20 pips and a trailing stop of 20 pips, and the price just moved in your favor by 20 pips. Then the stop loss would move to secure your trade at the entry, or breakeven, leaving 20 pips of room between it and the current price.

If the market starts to go against you, don't worry. Your trailing stop will not move. Instead, it will remain right where it is at break-even until the price hits it and takes you out of the market, or the price moves your way, so you're up by 40 pips. If the latter happens, then the trailing stop will move to secure 20 pips of profit so that even if you get taken out of the market, you have secured some money.

Other orders include:

- **Good 'Til Canceled** or **GTC:** Your broker won't ever cancel the order unless you give the order to do so.
- **Good for the Day** or **GFD:** Your order will remain active until the trading day is over.
- **One Cancels the Other** or **OCO:** This allows you to place two orders below and above the price (when one order becomes active, the other is canceled).
- **One Triggers the Other** or **OTO:** One order is only triggered if another order kicks in.

Placing Trades

Order executions vary from platform to platform and broker to broker. However, you need to be aware of a few things before placing your order, regardless of your trading method. First, your decision will be informed by the strategy you use to trade.

1. First, work out whether you're going to buy or sell a currency pair.
2. Go over your analysis and make sure that is the direction you want to trade, and you know where you want to get out at if the trade wins or loses.
3. Ensure you have multiple reasons for expecting the trade to play out the way you think it will. These reasons put together are called **confluence.**
4. Check your tools and indicators to be sure they're giving you the right signals.
5. Figure out your take profit target by using previous areas where price reacted strongly.
6. Choose your order type.
7. Enter your lot size, never risking more than 2 percent of your account balance per trade.
8. Set your stop loss and take profit levels before you pull the trigger.

By going through this list or something similar, you can structure your trades, so you're not just taking them based on blind luck, and you can prevent silly mistakes like buying a standard lot of USDJPY on a $100 account (it happens more often than you think).

Once the trade is on, you must monitor it. You don't have to sit at your charts and disregard every other aspect of your life. You can just set price alerts, so you know if the price has hit your stop loss (SL), your take profit (TP), or the level at which you want to go breakeven (BE). When you place your trades and your alert levels, do yourself a favor and walk away. Only come back if you get any alerts.

Finally, never move your stop loss. You should make sure you put it in a safe spot so that it definitely means the trade was invalid if it does get hit. When you move your stop loss, you're teaching yourself a terrible habit that will one day ruin you with a considerable loss.

Trading isn't about **always** being right, as you will learn later in this book. It's about being right enough times and having more than enough ammo to come back at it later when you're wrong. Whenever you feel like moving your stop loss or risking more money than you should, remember that "the markets can stay irrational longer than you can stay solvent." There's always going to be another setup. Walk away and try some other time again.

Chapter Three: Analyzing the Markets and Yourself

To trade, you need a strategy or a plan of action. To create a successful strategy, you need to become a researcher. You need to get all the information you can about the markets you will be trading and the influences on the assets' prices. This means you must learn how to analyze price action and market conditions.

The most common ways to analyze the markets are:

1. Fundamental analysis.
2. Technical analysis.
3. Market sentiment.

Fundamental Analysis

This process involves developing a trading strategy based on news and data that show the countries' economic strengths and weaknesses that affect their associated currencies.

If a country is doing well economically, its success should be apparent in the strength of its currency. Also, when a country's economy isn't so hot, you will see that reflected by weakness in its currency. In other words, everyone wants to buy the dollar when it's hot and drop it like it's hot when it's not—figuring out which currency is stronger than which will show you the best pairs to trade and which ones not to bother with because their currencies are equally strong (or equally weak).

The info you get to carry out this sort of analysis is known as fundamentals. All fundamental data involves news on all scales, from macroeconomic events to global issues and more local, national occurrences. You use fundamentals to determine the likely impact they will have on the currency markets and forecast possible trends. According to fundamental traders, when you can work out how the market will react, you can then plan your trades and capitalize on the volatility caused by these economic events.

Not all news events will move prices by hundreds of pips. Non-Farm Payrolls are so massive in their effect that even non-US currencies are affected (or at least, that used to be the case every time). Other events barely affect the price at all. Some websites show you the news events which have weight and the ones that don't. Generally, you should look out for the following data because they will rock your charts and might give you good trades after they have been released:

- Interest Rate Decisions
- Employment Rates
- Trade Balance Reports
- Retail Sales Figures
- Inflation Reports
- Gross Domestic Product Information
- Durable Goods Reports

- Speeches by Central Bank heads and presidents

You can use resources to track all this data, available online and in the news as well. You can also set up alerts to know when each event is about to occur or has occurred. You have the option of only getting notified when it involves the currencies you trade (because you don't have to trade every single thing your broker offers unless you want to go broke).

If you decide you want to be a fundamentals trader, then you should know which news releases to expect at the start of each week, or better yet, look them up over the weekend and plan for them. It will help you immensely if you journal your expectations, especially for the events you feel will have the most influence, so you can plan your trades.

Trading Fundamentals

When there is a news release, and it's in line with everyone's expectations, there won't be much movement in the prices of the pairs. However, suppose the news release results are significantly different from what everyone else expected. In that case, fundamental traders expect there's most likely to be a strong market reaction.

When the news release is significant, the market goes quiet for some minutes before it comes out, anticipating the figures. Then, shortly after the release of unexpected figures, the price will move explosively, but only for a very short period, and then the markets will usually correct themselves after.

If you want to trade news, you've got to have the best internet, a fast computer, and quick fingers. You also need a broker who doesn't widen the spreads too much. This is because the spreads are always wider than usual, just before and after a news release (no matter how excellent your broker is).

When trading **interest rates,** know that when the rates are up, the corresponding currency will rise. When trading **employment figures,** know that higher employment numbers mean more people in the workforce, which means a strong economy and a strong currency. When trading the **gross domestic product** figures, know that the higher they are, the stronger the currency.

Durable goods orders are a market of manufacturing power. Retail sales show how much people spend money in a country or don't. The latter two aren't as important as the events mentioned above.

Beware the "Funny Mentals"

One problem with trading news is that market volatility skyrockets to the point where you can see fifty or even hundred-pip movements in a matter of a second. If you can react that fast, then chances are you're a robot, and you don't know it. Prices change so rapidly, with wild fluctuations. You can't be sure your broker will be able to fill you in at the price you want because of this erratic behavior of price, and whether you might get filled at the very end of a move, with your stop loss too far away, because of the wide spread. This is known as **slippage,** and it's how many newbie accounts have gone bust.

The other issue with trading fundamentals, or "funny mentals," is that they aren't quite reliable. For instance, there have been too many times when news that should have been bullish for the dollar caused all USDXXX pairs to plummet at best or whipsaw back and forth for several hundreds of pips, leaving many new traders scratching their heads wondering where $99,999 of their $100,000 account just disappeared to.

Also, those who study price action and institutional order flow will tell you over and over that before the news is released, you can actually see where the price is going to go from just studying the charts. This is why I'm an advocate of the following kind of analysis.

Technical Analysis

Technical analysis is the study of price action and market structure to determine possible trends in the market. In other words, technical traders don't care what the news has to say. They only want to know when it's time for a news event so that they can secure trades that were running before that time. Or the traders want to make sure they don't put any trades at that same time.

Or they sit back and watch the Central Banks manipulate the price and take it where they expect it to go, so they can shadow them and make money when things settle down. The technical trader knows the significance of past prices and how they will likely show where the price will go in the future.

There are so many ways to analyze the charts, but one thing remains constant. You must understand price action. When you understand price action and the price arrives at a level it reacted to in the past, you will know if you should join the prevailing uptrend or downtrend or if you should expect a reversal. The technical trader knows how to make sense of the squiggly lines on the chart without needing to check in with Trump or LaGarde about where the Dollar or Euro will head next.

There are three kinds of technical traders:

- Those who rely on indicators, thinking that these bells and whistles move the price (spoiler alert: They don't).
- Those who understand chart patterns, using indicators to trade them.
- Those who only rely on price action, ignoring everything else.

You can be any of these three, provided you don't believe the hype that an indicator is what causes the price to move. Once you understand why price acts the way it does, you will only use them as confluence and not your sole reason for trading (if you ever use indicators, that is).

Market Sentiment

Market sentiment is about figuring out the ideas and feelings of other traders like you about the market. You want to know what they're likely to do and why. You want to work out what the herd mentality is about the pair you're looking at. Are traders bullish? Bearish? Neutral? This is what market sentiment seeks to figure out. It's not the easiest thing to understand or measure, but with experience, you'll start to figure out the answers for yourself.

What Kind of Trader Are You?

Figuring out your trading style isn't an easy thing, and it's not always a fixed choice. As a beginning trader, you will have to experiment with the various trading styles before you finally settle on a strategy and method that works for you and will not significantly change your lifestyle or drain your funds. You absolutely have to find out what kind of trader you are, though, as this will dramatically affect your trading results and how profitable or not you are in the long term.

So, we're going to help you figure out what works best for you. First, I'll get into the three styles of trading you should check out. Then we'll sink our teeth into the major ways in which they're different. Finally, we'll make a comparison, and then we can arrive at a hopefully clear conclusion about what kind of trader you want to be. But, again, even that decision need not be set in stone. I started out as a scalper, moved on to position trading, and then decided to day trade and scalp on the side. So maybe you'll have a mixture of styles. Let's see what all this scalping business is about.

Scalping

This is a trading style where the trader, called a "scalper," looks to profit from minimal asset price changes. The scalper opens a large number of trades or huge lot sizes in a single trading session, intending to get as many little wins as they can.

The scalper trades the markets with the shortest time frames possible, from the 1-minute chart to the 30, 15, and 5 second charts. For example, they could trade 2-pip Renko charts or 10-tick charts. The options are limitless but ultimately dependent on their scalping strategy. The scalper's trades usually only last a few seconds or minutes, but never more than a few hours. Also, the scalper requires higher leverage than other traders.

The whole point behind scalping is to get the most you can in the shortest amount of time you can, with the smallest movements possible. What makes the scalper profitable is that they use a substantial position. One way or another, they close their trades before the end of the day or session.

To be a scalper, you've got to be quick. There's no time to dawdle and overthink about whether your trade will play out. In extreme situations, you'll open up a trade and close it in a matter of seconds if there's enough movement in your favor… Or against you.

Because this trading style is so fast, you need precision with your entries and exits in time and price. In addition, you need a computer that won't fail you and backup internet for your internet. It sounds dramatic, but the last thing you want is to be hundreds or thousands of dollars in the hole for a trade you took just because your internet connection chose the perfect time to go off on you.

To trade as fast as you can with your scalping technique, you need to be on the lower time frames, from the five-minute charts and below. You want to wait for a powerful combination of reasons to get into a trade, from critical support and resistance levels to other things your indicator and price tell you. You cannot afford to take any setup that is not a high probability.

Finally, scalpers work well with indicators. Some don't use them, but if they help your strategy, you need to know that they're all telling you the same thing: Buy, or sell, or get out.

The indicators are split into support and resistance indicators (or "indis," in Forex-speak) and momentum indicators. Among the popular momentum indicators are the MACD (Moving

Average Convergence Divergence), the Stochastic Oscillator, the RSI (Relative Strength Index). The most common support and resistance (S&R) indis are moving averages, Keltner Channels, and Pivot Points.

To summarize, this trading style is about quick thinking. You'll get more setups than other traders. Also, as a successful scalper, your win rate needs to be higher than that of a regular trader because usually, what you risk and what you stand to gain are worlds apart, and you risk more than you earn. To make up for that, you need to win more trades than you lose. Your position size and win rate need to be high so that if and when you do lose, your winning trades cover all losers.

Managing your trades as a scalper means you can't take your eyes off the screen, usually. However, if you have a strategy that allows you to use pending orders, trailing stop losses, and so on, then you won't have to deal with that problem.

Day Trading

Many new traders think that scalping and day trading are the same, but they aren't. Both of them happen in a day, but there are still notable differences between them. The day trader opens and closes fewer trades than the scalper. They can open just one set up for the day, or two at the most, and be done with it.

Day traders and scalpers trade intraday, but the day trader is focused on getting the day's best opportunities and will hold on to their trade for a much larger profit goal than the scalper. So, the day trader will hold a trade for hours, but never more than a day. The ultimate goal of this kind of trader is to hold out for a larger piece of the pie with just one trade. This allows them to handle losses better than a scalper, even with a lower win rate.

As a day trader, the first thing you do is watch and wait for the price to get to significant levels on the charts where you see the potential to earn more pips than you're about to risk and where the trade is likely to go in your favor. After that, you need to be very patient as the price will move in your favor and then move against you, sometimes several times in a trading day or session.

You also must stick to your trading plan and never exit a trade sooner than you should have. If you do, you will eventually burn your account because you took a scalp trade when that wasn't your plan, and you're not trading the right strategy or lot size to win at scalping.

Your mission then is to seek out the best places to sell and buy an instrument in a day, and then make that trade and hold on to it until it hits your target. You'll still use some leverage, of course, but your lot sizes will be more reasonable. Your win rate may be as low as 30 percent, but as long as your winners are more significant than your losing trades, you can still come out on top.

The day trader has various kinds of analyses in their trading arsenal. For example, they can use a combination of indicators like the RSI and MACD, along with candlestick patterns and price action to work out the trends, resistance and support areas, and so on. They can also work with wave and chart patterns to get a better context of the marketplace.

Swing Trading

Swing traders don't just enter the market all day, every trading day. Instead, they enter and exit sporadically. They see a setup, get in and hold it for days or weeks on end. The point of swing trading is to look for intermediate setups to bag pips from. This is different from position trading, where you can hold a trade for weeks or even months.

The swing trader is different from the scalper and day trader because they use lower leverage than the other two. This isn't always the case, though, as some swing traders can go much higher in leverage. The swing trader also considers technical and fundamentals usually. I say "usually" because I knew some excellent swing traders who couldn't care less about the "funny mentals."

As a swing trader, your target is a lot larger, and you have to wait much longer than others for your trades to come to you. Some swing traders have to use wider stop losses (this is the case for most, actually), but you have some who have perfected the art of narrowing down their stop losses to less than ten pips so they can pull in several times more than that.

Some swing traders leave their trades on until just before the weekend, while others will hold on to their trades for weeks on end. Swing traders can work with the weekly, daily, four-hour, and one-hour charts. Here's how they might do that (although this isn't the rule for every swing trader):

- The higher time frames (daily, four-hour, and even monthly charts) are used to scout major support and resistance levels, as well as trends.
- The four-hour charts are used to scout for patterns that signify a setup is coming.
- The one-hour and four-hour charts are used for entries.

Traders who use Elliot Wave price theory, Fibonacci, and various price action patterns are likely to swing.

The Best Trader

Which of these three options is the best? There's no answer to that question. It all comes down to you. If you aren't quick to change your decisions, and you typically don't budge on significant choices you make unless there's good reason, then you might find success as a swing or position trader. (The latter group of traders hold for months and years and are more like investors than actual traders). If you have some patience, but not that much, try day trading or swing trading. If you're the kind who thinks on their feet and makes snap judgments, you might be a natural scalper. The only way to know for sure is to test them all out and see how you like it.

Scalping is a skill, and not just dumb luck. Experienced traders who have been in the markets for years can do this with ease. They understand how to work with the markets and have developed money and risk management skills to ensure their equity curve stays high.

The learning curve for the day trader and swing trader is steep as well, but the skills, emotional control, and experience are nowhere near the same as with scalping. So, swing trading and day trading is the best for beginners.

Ask yourself the following questions:

1. What style do I gravitate to the most?
2. What goals do I have? Do I want a little income on the side, or do I want to be a full-time trader?
3. What style do I prefer - technical analysis, fundamentals, or market sentiment analysis?
4. How much time do I have to enter, manage, and exit my positions?

More time means you can be more active and shorten your learning curve. It also means you can scalp if that's what you want to do. Swing trading is excellent for those who have full-time jobs because they can hold on for longer and only need to look at their charts for a few minutes each day. This isn't the case with day traders and scalpers.

Chapter Four: Lines, Bars, Candlesticks

Now it's time to talk charts. Charts are absolutely needed for you to do proper technical analysis. There are so many ways you can look at the price. You could use a line chart, a candlestick chart, or a bar chart. There are range charts, renko charts, heiken ashi charts... The list goes on, but we only need to focus on just the basics.

Time Frames

On your trading platform, you will notice that you have various time frames. For example, you get to see what price has done over the past five minutes if you select the five-minute time frame.

Lines

The line charts are straightforward. On your trading platform, all you'll see is one continuous line that shows the close price of each period of the time frame you've selected. There's not a lot to see with a line chart (if you're a newbie), but you will find it handy to assess the trends and breaks in market structure with enough screen time. The line chart works best for analysis on the higher time frames.

Bars

A bar chart has more information than a line chart. It shows you the OHLC (open, high, low, and close) of each period within your chosen time frame. The top of the bar is the high price, and the bottom is the low price.

In a bullish bar, the open price is the bottom dash on the left, while the close is the top dash to the right. The open price is the top left dash for a bearish bar, while the close price is the bottom right dash. Not a lot of people use bar charts at the beginning of their forex journey. However, if you'd like to try, but you find them confusing, just know the open is always to your left, and the close is to your right. Bearish bars have higher opens and lower closes than bullish ones.

Candlesticks

They're not the same as the ones you'd use on a romantic date, but they do bear some similarities to those. Called Japanese candlesticks, they show you the same open, high, low, and close of each period in a way that's easier on the eyes. **Always wait for the candle to close before taking your trade, so you don't get faked out. Likewise, never take a trade when a closed candle doesn't confirm it.**

A candlestick is made up of the body and the shadow or wick. The wick may be either on the upside, downside, both sides, or nonexistent as in a marubozu candle. Put together, they can show you patterns in price, so you know if it's time to reverse or if the present trend will continue. Candlestick patterns are powerful when they show up at critical levels.

The bodies are the filled-in areas of the candlesticks. The bearish candles are black or red, the bullish ones are white or green. The lines are sticking out of either end are the wicks or shadows. Your charting platform should have the option to change the colors. If you're using the popular MT4 platform, the candles will be lime and black.

However, if you prefer the traditional lime and red or blue and red of bullish and bearish colors, respectively, it's easy to adjust. Some traders use only one color for both so that they can really focus on price action.

When the bullish candle has a long body, that means there is a lot of buying presence or volume in that bar. When it's a bearish candle with a strong, long body, it indicates selling pressure. However, if you look at the chart above, you'll notice that you can see strong bearish and bullish candles that still wound up reversing. So, what gives? Forex is about having a statistical edge. We know that these candle behaviors imply certain things most of the time, **not all the time.**

When there is a long shadow or wick, it means that the price had pushed past the open or close price during that period. When the wicks are short, it shows traders tried to push the price in that direction, but they failed.

Long lower wicks show that there's bullish strength coming into the market in anticipation of higher prices. Conversely, **long upper wicks** show the bears are stepping into the market, potentially lowering the price.

Spinning tops are candles that have long wicks on both sides, with a petite body. They suggest that the price opened, tried to push up (or down) but failed, then tried to push down (or up) only to fail again. In terms of market sentiment, this is a clear mark of indecision between both bulls and bears.

A **marubozu** is a candle that has a long body (either bullish or bearish) with no wicks at all. This means that the open price of that period is equal to its lowest price (in a bullish marubozu), or the open price of that period is the same as the high (in a bearish marubozu).

A **doji** has a very short body like a line, and the open and close prices are pretty much the same. This could mean there's no volatility, or the market is pausing before another big move to continue its present trend (whether up or down) or reverse completely. If you notice a doji after a sequence of strong, long candles, that means buying strength is weakening. If you see it after strong selling pressure, that means the sellers are cooling off.

Candlestick Patterns

Two or more candlesticks can create patterns that let us know if the trend will continue or reverse. Unfortunately, there are too many candlestick patterns out there, so we will focus on just the ones you will find the most useful, mainly when applied to significant price levels.

Tweezers show up at the end of an extended downtrend or uptrend in the market and suggest that the market might be looking to reverse.

Engulfing candles can be bullish or bearish. With a bullish engulfing candle, the candle's body "engulfs" the previous candle. When these candles show up, you can expect the price to take off with strength in that direction.

Chart Patterns

To be an effective technical analyst, you should also be able to see the patterns in that chart that play out repeatedly. They let you know if the price is going to continue or reverse. They let you know when you should stay out of the market or get out of a trade. You can use these patterns along with candlestick formations to add more confluence to why you should (or shouldn't) take a trade.

Reversal and Continuation Patterns

You can find chart patterns in times of reversals or continuations. The way you interpret each one depends on several factors. Still, the bottom line is they'll let you know if you should expect the price to continue the present trend (as is the case with continuation patterns) or if the price is going to reverse (as reversal patterns indicate). These patterns can also show up in ranging markets, letting you know what will happen when the market stops ranging.

There isn't an exact science to these patterns, but with practice, you come to know where they form and why, and if they're valid to your setup. When you reach a certain level of proficiency, you will know which patterns are your bread and butter and which rob you to pay your broker.

Head and Shoulders

This pattern is a reversal pattern. It comes at the top of an uptrend or the bottom of a downtrend (inverse head and shoulders). These patterns have four parts to them, which, when present, could mean you're about to catch a massive move the other way.

An actual head and shoulder pattern will have a shoulder or swing high, then a higher swing which is the head, and then a swing high lower than the head, which forms the second shoulder. The last ingredient to this recipe is the neckline, which you will find by drawing a trend line to connect the swing lows of this pattern. This neckline acts as an area of resistance for you to sell from.

When the first shoulder is formed, price moves up to a new high (or down to a new low) then peaks as it creates a swing high (or low) before pulling back (or rising). The short retracement is then succeeded by a climb higher (or lower) before hitting an all-time high (low) for that period.

Then the market will pull back to make a new swing high (low) which sets up the head higher (or lower) than the shoulder. Price will then push back up to a level at or around the first shoulder and then pull back to create the second one.

It is at this point that the price then breaks the neckline to create the full pattern. You can enter on the break of the neckline, or better yet, wait for a pullback and a new swing to form to get a better entry with less drawdown. When you have less drawdown, trading just works out for you better psychologically.

You should keep the volume in mind when you're trading the head and shoulder pattern. Usually, the trading volume picks up at the break of the neckline and gives you extra confluence or confirmation about your bias.

To set your take profit for this trade, measure the distance between the neckline and head. Then take that exact measurement and apply it from the neckline down or up in your trade direction. This level is where you should take partial profits, trail your stops, or close the trade.

Symmetrical Triangles

These are great for illustrating ranging markets or a period where bulls and bears are indecisive about where to push the price next. Usually, when the price ranges or is in a triangle, it's also at a state of equilibrium, with equal supply and demand in the market.

You can use symmetrical triangles to help you work out when to get into the market. The pattern usually leads to a continuation of the previous trend. For instance, if the trend before the triangle formed was moving up, you can expect the triangle to break to the upside above the descending support line. On the flip side, if the trend was bearish, you can expect a downward break.

This doesn't work all the time, though - not just because not everything is accurate in Forex, but because **the market makers know these patterns and deliberately set them up for traders to hop on.** If you are a scalper, you might be able to get your pips and get out. If you're a day trader or a swing trader, then you might find it wiser to fade the moves. Since 99 percent of traders often lose money, it's smart to **not** do the same things that they all learn from the same textbook.

A meeting of two trend lines creates the triangle, one ascending and one descending. The lines ideally have the same slope and come together at the same point. Each swing high and swing low created (the lower highs and higher lows) grows closer, respecting the shape of the triangle. You'll notice that the trading volume is low at this time. Price will bounce back and forth between both lines, and as it gets close to the meeting point, there'll be a breakout.

To trade this one by the book, you can put a pending buy order above the descending trend line and a pending sell order below the ascending trend line. This way, whichever way it moves, you'll be triggered into the trade, and you can grab your pips. You could use an OCO order for this so that when one is activated, the other is canceled.

Ascending Triangles

These have a flat top that acts as resistance and an ascending trend line on the bottom that acts as support. A series of higher lows form the ascending trend line.

The pattern shows continuation and is seen as bullish. You can rely on the pattern a lot more when it shows up as part of an uptrend. Like with a symmetrical triangle, the price will bounce around both lines of the triangle, and then it will break to the upside. You can also find them in bearish market conditions, but they won't be as powerful. Also, keep in mind that price can break to the downside to fake you out.

To trade this, you can take the breakout to the upside by setting a buy-stop order above the resistance zone, or you could wait for the breakout to play out and then take the next swing low as your entry.

Descending Triangles

These are the opposite of ascending triangles in that they are indicative of bearish continuations. So, they show up in a downtrend. If they show up in an uptrend, you probably won't do so well trying to short them. The descending triangle has a flat bottom or support and a resistance trend line that slopes downwards, created by the progressively lower swing highs in that range.

Price will bounce between both lines until it finally breaks to the downside. Or it could break to the upside to fake you into a move and fake you out of some pips. To catch this move, set a sell stop below the support, or wait for the break and a brand-new swing high before you take a trade.

Flags and Pennants

These are continuation patterns as well, and they happen right after strong moves in price. After the strong move, there's a period of consolidation, and that's where you find the pennant or flag. When price forms a rectangle, it's called a flag. When it forms a triangle, it's called a pennant.

When the price moves powerfully in one direction, the market needs to pause for a bit to accumulate more orders in a range, and then it can continue up or down to its target. The pennant or flag is an excellent pattern for breakout traders to use. These patterns are either bullish or bearish. The bullish flags and pennants show up after a solid move to the upside, while the bearish ones happen after a strong downward push.

Wedges

Distinctly different from the wedgies you got in grade school, these patterns are created over much more extended periods than others. They can represent reversals or continuations, and they are shaped almost like symmetrical triangles. Again, there are **rising wedges** and **falling wedges.**

The rising wedge is created when the price starts to the range, bound by support and resistance lines that slope to the upside. You'll notice that the support line is a lot steeper than the resistance. Because of the higher lows, price forms faster than the higher highs. This is what gives the wedge its very distinct shape. So, when you catch a rising wedge, expect some serious movement to come.

When there's a rising wedge that comes after an uptrend, it suggests there might be a reversal coming up soon. But, on the other hand, when it forms as part of a downtrend, then there's a chance the downtrend will continue. In other words, this pattern is bearish because it always leads to a downward push, regardless of the trend. With the falling wedge, you can expect that price will push to the upside no matter the trend.

Rectangles

These chart patterns happen when the price is bound by parallel lines, which act as support and resistance. Here, the market is at equilibrium, which is the same as a consolidation or ranging market, as I've mentioned before. This pattern shows indecision about where the price is heading. Some traders love this trading pattern because they can short at the top of the range and go long at the bottom. But consolidations don't last.

Eventually, there will be a breakout or a fake-out to one side and then a true breakout the other way. The smarter way to avoid being faked into the wrong move is to wait for the price to really break out of the rectangle, retest a new level, and show a willingness to continue in that direction with a strong close.

Price movement can follow the direction of the trend before the rectangle forms, but you know what I'm about to say again. Not everything in Forex is.... You know the rest. Just keep in mind that when a breakout happens, the move can be very massive. So, wait for the price to pull back to the point of origin of the explosive movement, show signs of finding support (or resistance), create a new swing low (or high), and then get in a trade.

Double Tops, Double Bottoms, Triple Tops, and Triple Bottoms

These are chart patterns that show reversals. When you see them, there's a chance that the trend is about to shift dramatically. For example, after an uptrend in a double top formation, the price will form a high. Then it will pull away, attempt to create a higher high, and then fail at or before (or just slightly above) the previous swing high. The break of the most recent swing low is extra confirmation, so you can wait to get in on the first swing high that forms after that swing low violation.

With a triple top, the same attempt to push up higher happens two more times before the price pushes the other way sharply. You can enter after the next swing high formed (or go to a lower time frame to find one you can use to join the trend).

When it's a double bottom, the price hits an all-time low after a prolonged downtrend. Next, it pushes away from a level, creating support. Then price retraces and then pushes down once more. It fails to go further than the first low or only manages to push just a little after it or even fails to hit the first low.

Then, price rallies. The break of the last swing high created validates this pattern. You can take long trades after the price has pulled back a bit and formed a new swing low after the violation or scale down to lower time frames to join the move.

Remember to only look for these after the market has been trending for a long time. You will get much better results if you wait for them to play out on the 4-hour chart. Even if you're a scalper, you could set a price alert for that level, and then when the level is hit, you can go down to lower time frames to hunt for trades. Remember, you shouldn't take any trade until the market structure on the lower time frame breaks the other way, showing you that the price on that time frame is ready to line up with the higher time frame premise you have.

A Final Note on Trading Patterns

So, you open up your chart, and hey, there's that head and shoulders pattern you just learned about. Without waiting, you pull the trigger on a sell trade. It will go down for sure, so you think. Next thing you know, the price begins to go up, pulling away from your entry.

You can't stand that you're now negative ten pips, maybe even more. This isn't how it was supposed to go, you think. So, you close the trade. Or you get taken out of the trade because the price hits your stop loss. But then, a few hours later, the price **does** push down as you thought it would. So, what went wrong with that trade?

The setup was fine. Your entry, however, could use some work. If you want to make it in Forex, you need to master the fine art of patience. Money always moves from the impatient to the patient. Breakout traders can be profitable, but the trader who has ten times more of a chance to make money is the one who always gets in on the pullbacks.

When price moves, it does one of three **other** things, besides go up, down, or sideways. These are the three phases of price in motion in an established trend:

1. Push
2. Pullback
3. Pause

Breakout traders get in on the push, which is after the move has long begun. This means they have to have wider stop losses and are likely to suffer drawdown when the price enters phase two of its movement, the pullback or retracement. Now, you should still wait before you put in your order because you have no idea how far back the price will retrace. After the price is done retracing, it will pause for a couple of candles, maybe more.

If you're adept at reading price action and you notice the price is at a significant level (old support or resistance on higher time frames, round figure prices, and 500 prices), then you could get in here. However, the best thing for you to do is wait for one candle to close strong in the direction of the trend. This candle will be your trigger candle, and it will let you know where to put your stop loss.

Chapter Five: Technical Trading Strategies

Let's Talk Trends

You might have heard it said that the trend is your friend. When it comes to trading, this is so true. Don't try to fight it, or you will get burned. You should understand the conditions of the market before you get into a trade. Then, when you know if the market is pushing up or down, you can get in and enjoy the ride with it. Remember, retail money doesn't even touch what the banks trade with, so why try to fight them by picking tops and bottoms when you could simply ride along with them?

The market does one of three things:

- Push up (uptrend)
- Push down (downtrend)
- Consolidate or move sideways (Move up and down within a fixed range)

In an uptrend, the price makes higher highs and higher lows. To easily recognize an uptrend, you can draw a line connecting the higher lows together. As long as the price stays above that line (called a **trend line**), you should only look for buys.

In a downtrend, the price makes lower lows and lower highs. To make the downtrend clear to you, you can draw a trend line that connects the lower highs to one another. As long as the price continues to trade below the trend line, you're good to sell.

When the market ranges, price is still moving up and down but only in a defined area. This is also called **consolidation** or a "sideways moving market."

Sometimes, the price will have issues with breaking up and past a certain level. That area where price keeps running from is known as **resistance**. When price can't break through a specific area on the downside, and it only keeps bouncing away, that area is called **support.**

This will become more important to you later. Generally, ranging markets don't have a clear directional bias, and price doesn't have to get all the way to the top or the bottom of the consolidation on each move.

One fantastic tool that can help you figure out your trading decisions is Fibonacci, which you can use to figure out trending markets. The better tools to use when the market is ranging are support and resistance levels and pivot points.

In a trending market, the price continues to make new lows (downtrend) or new highs. But price doesn't just shoot all the way down or up. Regardless of what direction it's trending in, it will make a little move the other way. The small movement is called a **retracement** or a **pullback.** When the price resumes the trend after the retracement and breaks the most recent higher high or lower low, it creates a **swing**. You can also call the lows and highs "swing lows" and "swing highs." In a way, you could say these swings are little supports and resistances too. When the trend is valid, the price shouldn't break the previous swings. If it does, that's a break in market structure and could signify a change in trend direction, so you'd better not try to trade against the trend, or you will get burned.

More on Support and Resistance

Support and resistance are vital to technical analysis. Traders have many opinions about what counts as support and resistance and whether they work well for trading. One of the reasons for this debate is that sometimes, you'll find that price blasts through these levels, and other times, they won't quite reach them before turning around and heading the other way. The best traders know that support and resistance isn't a line on the chart but an area.

When you factor that into your trading, you will see more profitable moves, and you can get in on the move earlier than others who are indecisive about what direction to trade in.

Support and resistance form as a result of market activity and general market sentiment. When traders sense the price is moving too fast to the upside or overbought, the market resists further buying. The consensus is that any price above that level would simply be too high, and no one is willing to buy at a premium when they would rather buy at a discount. Here's the thing, though: **the price is at a premium.** There's no demand but plenty of supply. So, buyers liquidate their positions, and bears rush in at those levels, sending it down, creating resistance.

The same thing happens when the price can't push any lower than a level. It's the market sentiment that the market is oversold and shouldn't go any lower than that. No one wants to sell at a discount because they'd lose money. So, sellers liquidate their positions, bulls rush in, and that buying pressure confirms the area price ran up from as support.

Support and Resistance: Market Maker Style

These moves could lead to insane explosions the other way or just a bit of retracement. If you want to trade them like a pro, think as the market makers do. Most people learn to sell at resistance and buy at support. The buyers put their buy stops below the support levels. If you were a bank, what would you do? Gun for the stop losses, of course! This is why support and resistance *seem* not to work. The big boys have the funds to drive the price down to those lows. When they do that, two things happen:

- Breakout traders (traders who like to trade the break of support and resistance as continuation moves to

their respective directions) are induced to take sell positions.
- Buyers who had their stop losses placed at those levels are tagged out.

Now the buyers (who were actually right) are scared to jump back in for a buy, while sellers are getting greedy and placing their stop losses above the broken support. So, what do the banks do when they've gotten enough sellers? Remember, they are the **liquidity providers.** Unfortunately, the "liquidity" is dumb money and other hedge funds that don't know what they're doing.

So, when dumb money is selling below that support level, the smart money is buying from them. When the big boys have enough liquidity, they push the prices all the way back up again, gunning for the liquidity pockets at the next swing high.

You can repeat this same scenario for the resistance side. Price rallies past resistance, and everyone thinks they should buy. Stop losses are hit, buy stops are triggered. The smart money drove the price above that level, and there, they sell to every willing buyer. Once they have amassed enough liquidity, what do they do? They drive the price the other way, gunning for the next pocket of liquidity at the next swing low.

Now, remember what I just shared with you about market structure? The question is, how do you know when to get in on these moves? You want to look for the market structure to break and get back in line with your bias *after* the price has shot through the "resistance" and "support" levels. In forex, the most profitable traders are the ones who know how to sit on their hands and wait for confirmation before pulling the trigger. Only amateurs try to catch falling knives. The best of traders wait for the market to show its hand and then respond accordingly. They trade what they see, not what they think or feel.

Pivot Points

You can use pivots to work out support and resistance levels that are valid and might show you a genuine opportunity to anticipate a change in price action. They offer you levels where price might reverse or targets the price must hit before you can accept a breakout of support and resistance as valid.

There are various ways to calculate pivot points, but you can just let your charting platform handle that for you automatically. It still doesn't hurt to understand how it arrives at those points, though. The most common way to calculate them is by using the five-point system, where the high, low, and close are added and then divided by three.

Pivot Point = (High + Low + Close) /3.

Support 1 = (Pivot Point x 2)

Resistance 1 = (Pivot Point x 2)

Support 2 = Pivot Point - (High - Low)

Resistance 2 = Pivot Point + (High - Low)

Pivot Points in Day Trading

Some scalpers take significant positions and get in and out of trades after just a few minutes, only looking for two to three pips per trade. Then there are day traders, who have trades that last a few hours, or a couple of days, tops. Swing traders can hold their positions for days, while position traders can hold for weeks and months.

You have to work out what kind of person you are to figure out which works best for you. If you're patient and don't change your mind easily, stick to swing trading and position trading on higher time frames from the 4-hour chart and up. If you're a scalper, you could use the 1-minute, 5-minute, or even tick charts. The day trader can use the 15-minute chart up to the 4-hour chart.

If you're a day trader, you're going to love pivot points. They let you know strong support and resistance areas in the market, and you can expect big moves from these levels. It's either the price will rip right through these levels or will reject them for massive moves.

Pivot points help you work out when a trend is likely to occur. When price breaks below a pivot point, you can expect a downtrend to form, possibly. In the same way, if it breaks above, you can expect an uptrend. Remember, you should only ever buy at a discount and sell at a premium. If the price is below the central pivot point, then this is an excellent time to consider looking for longs if the general trend of the market is up on a higher time frame.

If the higher time frame (H4 and up) seems to be bearish, then you should only look for shorts on lower time frames at the resistance areas so that you're selling at a premium. Remember, you want the bullish market structure on the lower time frame to break and change to bearish before selling.

When buying, wait for the bearish trend on a lower time frame to break and become bullish. Understand that what you think of as a trend on the lower time frames could be just a retracement on the higher ones. If you frame your trades based on higher time frames, you will have more winners than losers, and massive ones at that.

Please note that pivot points are recalculated each day, as they rely on the results of the day before. So, this is a short-term indicator. The smart call would be to use the higher time frames to plot these points and then stalk those levels on the lower time frames until you get a break of structure the correct way, and you have other confluence in the form of candlestick formations, and so on.

Pivots for Entries and Exits

These points are also handy as an indication of when your trade should start and when you should close your positions or take the bulk of them off the market.

Say price pushes and breaks past the pivot point. This could be your entry signal. Then you could set your stop loss just above the pivot point, making sure it's above the most recent swing high, so you don't get tapped out prematurely. The first support level can be your target (or the first resistance level, if you're buying).

If you don't set a take profit and would rather trail your stop, you could decide to get out if you notice that price has continued past that support level, or you could close part of your position and move your stop to break even so that the trade is risk-free. Then the next support level would be your next target (or the next resistance level, if you're buying).

When you're strategic about how you enter and exit with the help of pivots, you will find that you take advantage of the pips the market offers you, and you also get added peace of mind since you don't have to worry about what to do to manage your trade.

When it comes to pivot points, you should have some caution as you trade. You can't predict the markets. So please don't assume that the market must respect all pivot points. Some days, it will play nicely by the rules. Other days, it acts like a teenager who just hit puberty and wants to rage against the machine. So don't go betting your future Lambo on one trade, thinking that will make you rich. That's not how this works.

If the price is just hovering around a pivot point, then you might not be able to tell where it's going. There's a deadly effective fix for that. Most people don't use it, but I'm giving you this one for free. Sit on your hands. If that doesn't work, just walk away. Later, when the market has shown a clear push to one direction and a refusal to break the swing that caused that push, you can hunt for a new setup. Then, when the price returns to the origin of the push and refuses to break the swing, you can take trades in the push direction.

Volume

You know what volume is, and I mentioned before that it's crucial. It's the number of trades going on in the market at any given time. It also lets you know whether the market is interested in sending a pair to the moon or the abyss.

Your charting software should offer you volume levels if it's a good one. You can find them at the bottom of your chart. If you're using good old MT4, just hit CTRL + L, and you should see the levels at the bottom of your chart.

Now here's the other thing about the volume I neglected to mention until now. There's no accurate way to measure it in Forex because the sheer number of the trades that are placed daily is ridiculous. Moreover, there's no central organization that can monitor the number of transactions. That said, market makers know the approximate transaction volumes at all times, and we can track them.

Each volume bar at the bottom of your chart shows you how much trading activity went on during that period (in our case, each volume bar shows the volume for four hours of trading). The bars also let you know whether there were more sellers than buyers or vice versa.

You should always keep an eye on volume, as it can add confluence to the trade setups you consider or can help you back out of a trade that would have been a loser. When there's movement in price along with a comparably higher trading volume than usual, then you can trust that move a lot more than if the levels were relatively lower than normal. In practical terms, always check to see if the volumes support your analysis.

The volume moves in line with the actual trend of the market. So as the trend blossoms and gathers momentum in one direction, there will be an increase in volume, which confirms that there truly is a lot of money moving that way, and you can decide to join in on that when price offers you a retracement for a better entry. Don't just go short or long because the volume bar was strong. Always get into your trades at a retracement, or at least right after the push phase of the move resumes after the price has shown it's done pulling back.

When the volume goes down, that means that trend is about to end, or it's pausing at least. So, it's an excellent time to take out some money from the market and make sure any running trades won't be a risk or possible loss, no matter what happens next.

Chapter Six: Moving Averages

A moving average is an indicator that lets you smooth out the ups and downs of price over a set period so that you can tell what the currency pair has been up to. Usually, a price chart shows all the details when it comes to price fluctuations. All this detail is not a bad thing if you know what to look for, but when it's a lot, it makes it hard to see when there's a trend being formed or when a setup for a good trade is happening.

With the moving average, you can smooth out the price fluctuations by plotting only the average price values, so it looks a lot smoother.

When you plot a moving average on your chart, it is easier to tell it's a downtrend because the price action is averaged out, and the jagged closes you'd find on a line chart are fewer. Sure, moving averages are lagging indicators (every indicator is a lagging indicator, actually, since they all follow the price). Still, you don't need to be the first in a trade to be profitable.

The moving average is calculated based on the average closing prices for a pair over the last "x" number of periods. A "period" could be the last 5 candles or the last 200. You get to decide. The higher the period you use, the smoother the action will look on the chart. The smoother it is, then the slower it will react to the price fluctuations in the short term. The more rugged the line is, the closer it is to real-time price.

There are different kinds of moving averages. You have the simple moving average. In Forex-speak, it's called the SMA. Then there's the exponential moving average, known as the EMA. There's also the smoothed moving average, also called SMMA for short, and the LWMA or linear weighted moving average. Fun fact: If you set up the last one to a period of 1, what you'll see is the exact same thing as a standard line chart of price in real-time. For the purposes of this book (and making pips), we'll focus on just the SMA and EMA.

The Simple Moving Average

This is the most straightforward average of them all in terms of calculation. The math behind it is to add "x" number of price closes and then divide them by "x." The value you get is dependent on the periods you set.

To calculate a 14 period SMA on a five-minute chart, you'd take the close prices of each of the last 14 5-minute periods or candles and then sum them up. Then you'd divide the number you get by 14. Fortunately, you don't have to work all this out on your own.

Your charting platform has got you covered and will plot a line to show you the value of the 14 SMA. Still, it's good to know the idea behind moving averages so that you can figure out how to make them work for you in your trading, depending on the settings you use.

Again, the moving average is a lagging indicator that only gives you clear hindsight of what price has done in the past. So don't think of it as a predictor of price or a crystal ball you can use to see where it goes next. Nothing is 100 percent accurate in Forex, and anyone who tells you so is trying to steal your money.

That said, these moving averages are really great to help you highlight **probable** emerging trends. I say "probable" because, for the umpteenth time, nothing is a hundred percent accurate in Forex. As you gain more experience with this indicator, you'll learn how to use it along with your analysis of the charts to spot good trading setups to take advantage of.

The SMA is a great way to get a bird's-eye view of what's happening in the markets, but sometimes when the price makes a rapid spike of several pips above its usual daily range, then you can't trust what the averages are saying. This is especially the case with the smaller time frames.

If you try to trade with the averages after a considerable spike many pips up or down, then you're going to find yourself in tears. So, a good rule of thumb is to go on the higher time frame to take a look at what price is really doing, or better yet, stay out of the markets until the next day when prices should have corrected.

The Exponential Moving Average

The EMA addresses some of the SMA issues, being that the latter can be a tad too slow. EMAs react to the price a lot faster so that when a price spike happens, its calculation accounts for the rapid price change. You can still get false signals with this, but it's less rampant than with the SMA.

EMAs are calculated by placing more focus on the values of the recently closed candles and less emphasis on the ones further back in time. This allows you to have a lot more accuracy as you watch what's going on with the charts in the short term. EMAs are a lot more responsive than SMAs, and a lot of traders prefer to use them. That doesn't mean the SMA has no value, as its slow reaction can keep you out of false moves.

How to Use Your Moving Averages

Moving averages are a great addition to your strategy when you know how to use them. When the moving average is moving up and is below the actual value of price, then that means there's an uptrend underway. When the moving average is heading down, and the price is below it, there's a downtrend in play.

Hang on. If it's really that simple, why isn't everyone making money in Forex? Well, there are so many reasons, but I'll focus on the topic at hand. The thing is, moving averages aren't always straightforward. For instance, if you look at both images, you'll notice that there are times when price pierces through the moving averages in the other direction, only to resume its original trend.

To combat the problem of false signals, one thing you can, and should, do is to use price action. Wait for a break in a significant swing high or low, a retest of the broken swing, and then a push away from that level before you validate the change in trend shown by your moving average.

These false breaks happen a lot, and if you don't understand price action and only use one moving average, your trading account will be whipsawed into a margin call. The false breaks are usually caused by some unexpected news or an event that causes the market some brief excitement before it settles. Every time there's news, the price may move erratically, but in the end, it will always go back to its original trend.

Since moving averages react ever so slowly to price, you might find that the line is on the wrong side of the price, which makes you think there's a reversal. But, of course, you'll fall for this trick less when you choose to keep your eyes on the price first, using the moving average to only add confluence to your setups.

Besides learning market structure and price action, traders use more than one moving average to keep themselves out of false moves and get more reliable ideas about what price might do next.

Plot two moving averages on your chart if you're struggling to work out which moves are fake and which aren't. This way, you'll have a more unambiguous indication of the present trend in price. One moving average will need to be slower than the other for this to work. The faster one will allow you to take setups in line with the trend shown by the slower one. In an uptrend, the faster MA will be above the slower one, while in a downtrend, the slower one will be above the quicker.

Whatever you do, don't just trade the crossover of two moving averages. Instead, always wait for the price to pull back and show a readiness to resume trends. This is because crossovers can be misleading too, and in range, market conditions moving average crossovers are unhealthy for your account balance. We'll talk more about crossovers in a bit.

Moving Averages for Momentum

You need to be able to tell the price momentum at any given time. Momentum is a fancy way of describing the strength with which price is moving. You can use moving averages to work out the market momentum. The way to do this is with various moving averages applied to different time frames.

For instance, the shorter-term momentum is evident when you use a moving average period of 20 or less. For the mid-term momentum, any period from 21 to 100 is acceptable. As for the long-term momentum, use periods above the 100 or the classic 200-period moving average. This means you'll have at least three moving averages on your chart.

When you have the short-term moving average above the other two slower ones, then this means you have bullish conditions in the market, especially when the fastest one pulls away from the others. Conversely, when the market is bearish, you'll have the reverse condition playing out on your chart.

Trading MA Crossovers

You can use the way two moving averages work with each other to work out your buys and sells. You could even use three moving averages. In this case, the slowest moving average lets you know if you should focus only on buying or selling, while the faster two show you when you should start looking for trades as they cross back in the same trend shown by the slowest one.

When the fastest EMA crosses the slower one to the upside, that's called a **bullish crossover**. When it crosses the slower one to the downside, it's a **bearish crossover**. When you have the short-term moving average above the other two slower ones, then this means you have bullish conditions in the market, especially when the fastest one pulls away from the others. Conversely, when the market is bearish, you'll have the reverse condition playing out on your chart.

Moving Averages as Dynamic Support and Resistance

Moving averages can be used as support and resistance, and they can work even better for this purpose than you eyeballing the chart. Why? Because while everyone sees something different on their charts and has subjective views on what makes support and resistance, the moving average is drawn by its price, which means its objective. It may lag, but in this sense, it doesn't lie. Go over the charts posted here and notice areas where the average acted as resistance or support to price.

Moving Averages for Entries

You can use the moving average to work out your entries into a trade. For example, say you had a good setup, but you were late getting into the trade. However, the price is still at a discount (for a buy) or a premium (for a sell), so you want to get in at a reasonable price with a stop loss that isn't wider than needed.

When the price crosses back down the moving average in line with the trend, and you get a candle close below the average, that is when you should pull the trigger. For now, if you're trading on the majors and other pairs with low spreads, you can get away with a ten pip stop if you enter trades this way on the fifteen-minute and even five-minute charts. As you gain more experience and become more confident in your trading, you can actually fine-tune your stop loss to be even lower than that. What happens when you take trades based on higher time frame targets with lower time frame entries? You rake in more pips than the average trader. The only thing that could possibly stand in the way of you making money is your emotions, specifically greed and fear. Greed makes you take positions too large for your account. Fear makes you cut trades too early. Learn to sit on your hands, and you will do better than most.

Moving Average Ribbons

A moving average ribbon is made up of various moving averages plotted with different periods on your chart. The idea behind using ribbons is that rather than using just one or three, you've got a whole bunch, from about 6 of them to 16, or even more. It might seem like a lot, but multiple moving averages can tell you everything you need to know about the strength of the trend, upcoming reversals, chances to enter new trades, and more.

Looking at the ribbon, the trader can work out the trend's strength by looking at the expansion that as occurred, the smoothness and alignment of the averages, as well as important support and resistance areas to keep an eye on.

The averages in a moving average ribbon depend solely on the trader's discretion. Some traders love to use about 6 or 8 simple moving averages, all set 10 periods apart from one another. Some use even more, from the 50 to 200 periods, and more in between. The longer-term averages help you identify the overall trend. Some traders use linear weighted moving averages for their ribbons, and others stick with the exponential. It all comes down to your preference.

If you want your moving average ribbon to be more or less responsive, you can adjust the number of periods you use, or you could change the kind of moving average you use. Remember, exponential averages react faster than the simple ones, and the shorter the periods you set, the quicker they will react to price action.

Ribbon Trading

When the moving average ribbon expands, that means there's a potential trend beginning. When you notice the moving averages getting wider apart and fanning out, that condition is called **ribbon expansion.** It could mean that the trend is coming to an end.

It's like the moving averages are all magnets drawn to each other by price action. They don't like being far apart for long, so the price will cause them to close the gaps anytime that happens.

When the moving average ribbon is contracting, that could also signal a change in the trend. This is called **ribbon contraction.** When the price has moved significantly in one direction for a while, the shorter-term moving averages will start to converge. The longer-term moving averages will join as well, but slower. If you add that convergence along with price action, you just could catch the start of a new, monstrous trend the other way.

When the moving average ribbon has all averages parallel to one another, a strong trend is underway. You don't want to buck that if you're a reversal trader. It is best to wait for the convergence to start and then use other methods to see if you're right about the trend change.

Alternatively, you could choose to get in on the trend by buying the dips if the market is moving up or selling the rallies if the market is moving down. Remember to apply the push-pull back-pause philosophy to your entries to make them tighter.

You should always watch the space between all the moving averages. Sadly, new traders tend to ignore this and only ever focus on the twists and crossovers, nothing more. So, while you should keep a finger on the pulse of the shorter-term moving averages as they cross below or above the longer-term ones, you should definitely keep an eye out for the spacing between them as well.

The position of the longer-term moving averages relative to the shorter-term ones will show you the trend direction, whether that's up, down, or neutral. The space between the averages indicates the trend's strength, whether strong, weak, or neutral.

Chapter Seven: Spotting Trade Setups

The professional trader needs to know how to spot a trade opportunity and apply their trading plan to take advantage of it. Traders take their time to figure out what's happening in the market and then strategically position themselves to take advantage of each chance they see to take pips out of the market.

Your Trading Routine

Make time to analyze the market. First things first, you must examine the currency pairs you want to trade. You can't just hop out of bed first thing in the morning and say, "Yup, I'm feeling lucky. Just going to go short on the Dollar CAD with max lots. YOLO!" If you think this is how that works, you might want to stop following those Instagram traders and focus on improving your skills.

The more often you analyze the market, the better you'll get at telling where it's likely to go and what it's expected to do, which means you will paradoxically need less time to look at the charts with time. You should keep yourself up to date on what happened in the markets day after day, as it's easier than trying to soak up information that spans many days.

So, before you take up trading, think long and hard about your routine and how much time you can realistically spend on the charts. If you only have a few minutes or so a day, you should focus on just a couple of currency pairs. If you have more time, you can look at more.

Be willing to spend an hour each day to look at your charts and keep track of news and other events if you trade fundamentals. Even if you don't know when the news events are coming so that you're prepared to manage running positions as needed, and you don't place a trade right when there's important news, and your spreads go crazy, losing you money.

In your trading routine, you should consider the following:

- Key support and resistance levels on higher time frames.
- Multiple time frame analysis to learn where the lower time frames are at relative to what's happening on the higher ones.
- Daily and weekly candle closes and price action.
- Economic data on the currencies you trade, which comes out overnight or while you were away from the charts.
- The possible impact of upcoming news events on the price of your chosen pairs.
- General market sentiment and commentaries to glean what every other trader is thinking and planning.

Is this a lot to fit into an hour? At first, perhaps. Still, as you do this more often, you will find your flow, and it will go faster for you.

Multi Time Frame Analysis

If you open up a currency pair on various time frames, the differences in the price action immediately jump out at you, but at their core, they're essentially telling the same story about what price has done, just on different time frames.

The highest time frame gives you the broad strokes along with the vital areas to look at, the middle one tells you where the price is at and what it might be doing next, and the smallest time frame (H1 in this example) is where you should be hunting for your entries.

Multiple time frame is not really that complicated, and it gets easier the more you look at the charts with different time frames. With time, you'll be able to tell that if you jump from the daily chart to the 5-minute chart, you should see a double bottom or a wedge that formed. There's really no other way to learn this stuff than to put in the work.

So, on your charting platform, mark out the most recent highest high and lowest low on the daily time frame for your pairs. Then, highlight all the price actions that took place in that range on the higher time frame. Note the swing points and areas where price violently moves away from. Highlight those separately as well.

Then, drop down to a smaller time frame, and see what played out at those key levels. Really look out for breaks in market structure, chart patterns, engulfing candles, and more.

Then drop down to an even lower time frame to work out what happened. Your brain will start to get used to the patterns and see things you might have missed before. Spend time doing this exercise, and you will see for yourself how useful it is.

Even if you decide you're going to scalp the one-minute charts, here's a piece of advice that will put you way ahead of millions of losing traders – always check the monthly, weekly, and daily candles and price action in general. They will show you where the most critical levels to focus your trading on are.

The power and accuracy of technical analysis on the higher time frames is a perfect edge to have in your trading. So please, never skip this. Don't keep your focus on one tree and miss the whole forest because it'll hurt you badly in the long run. Resistance and support are taken out like so much nothing on the lower time frames.

Patterns are invalidated like they never even existed, too. However, when you trade in line with a higher time frame bias, your trading will be dead on, mostly, and you can pull in more money than most with a defined risk per trade.

The thing about weeklies and dailies is that their levels don't fluctuate as often as the lower time frames. You can trust them, and you don't have to update those levels incessantly.

To see the power of trading in line with the higher time frames rather than the daily, check out each currency pair one every time frame and notice how much more explosive price patterns are when they show up on the higher time frames than on the lower ones. You get several opportunities to enjoy hundreds of pips over and over, thanks to using the daily chart or higher.

The Importance of Trend Lines

Trend lines are outstanding, as long as you keep adjusting them as price makes new swings for you to use. To work out support and resistance levels that coincide with trend lines, just connect swing highs and lows together. For ascending trend lines that show support, draw your trend line from the lowest and most recent swing low to the highest and most recent swing low.

The descending trend line, which acts as resistance, connects the highest most recent swing high to the lowest most recent swing high. You should always draw your trend lines from left to right.

Always remember that the value of a trend line over time will adjust along with the price. When you find an upward trend line, the value will be higher later on. When you find a downward one, the value will go down over time.

You can use the trend lines to place your orders based on your trade bias. However, trend lines can be broken, so keep that in mind. When that happens, you could simply hop to a lower time frame and see how to get in with the new trend. Whatever you do, always draw your trend lines on higher time frames, from the four-hour chart and onwards.

There are several ways to trade this line. First, you can trade away from it, letting it act as support (or resistance) when price hits it after a down move (or up to move). Second, you could wait for the price to break it and then break back in so you can fade the fake-out and get your pips.

Or you could choose to follow the breakout if you believe the exchange price should shoot through and continue in a new trend. Finally, you could use the trend line to get you into an already ongoing trend if you missed the start by selling on the pullbacks to it and taking profits at the most recent swing high or low.

The Lows and Highs of Trading

You could choose to focus on the highs and lows of a period as support and resistance. To find these levels from the highs and lows is just to notice the highest prices and lowest prices, but allow some wiggle room of about 5 to 15 pips because brokers all have different price feeds and spreads, and you want to make sure you're not knocked out of a trade.

Looking at the daily candles, you can easily spot the most critical highs and lows. However, on smaller time frames, it's never evident which ones matter and which ones don't. Just look for areas on the chart where there has been a significant movement away from.

As a rule of thumb, the sharper price moves away from a level, the more critical that level is. By "sharper," I mean price doesn't dawdle, and the candle or series of candles tend to be larger-bodied than usual for that currency on that time frame. By the same token, the slower price moves away from a level, the less important it is. So, you can look out for long wicks on your lower time frames when searching for signs that an old high just might be resistance, or an old low is acting as support.

Here's a quick note on trading algorithms and **expert advisors** (who aren't actual people but just a programmed trading system). A lot of them work with the breaks of old highs and lows. You can also use those breaks to give you trade signals, but to use them, you must wait for the candlestick of the time frame you're observing the level at to close beyond the low or high in question. For instance, some systems want a break and close above a high or a low before going long or short. That is what works best for short-term strategies. A longer-term system will need the daily low to break with a closed daily candle before shorting. This is just one more way to use the close of a period to confirm that a trend line or support and resistance break is indeed valid. When you enter your trade, make sure you have a stop loss in place if that is not a valid trade.

Fibonacci Retracements

On your charting platform, you should have several Fibonacci tools. You're interested in the Fibonacci retracement, to be specific. Draw them once there's been a significant movement in price that is clear as day, and then the price starts to pull back in the other direction.

When the daily Fibonacci levels break, this could be a significant opportunity for you, providing you with a trading signal. Also, Fibonacci retracements are excellent levels to take profits at before price comes back to take back all the pips you got and then some. Use these levels to place your stop losses as well.

One level to always look out for when it comes to Fibonacci is the 76.4 retracement level. It will give you turning points in price, especially with the more volatile GBP crosses, GBPUSD, and Gold.

Please keep in mind that you can draw fibs wherever you want to, but they are only as significant as the size of the huge, impulsive move. The stronger and more momentous the push to the upside or downside, the more importance the Fibonacci levels (fib levels) will have regarding your trading.

So, you would do well to draw your fibs on the daily charts so you can find the most important movements in price to place your fibs on. To draw fibs on a downtrend, you should connect the highest swing high of the range you're working with to the lowest swing low formed after price makes a pullback.

When drawing fibs in an uptrend, connect the lowest swing low of the range you're working with to the highest swing high *after* the price has started to pull back down.

Momentum, Timing, Entries, and Exits

You should study the momentum of price to help you figure out the timing of your trade for entries and exits. You don't want to get in a trade and have to sit in it for longer than you're used to because there wasn't enough momentum to send it your way. Also, you don't want to sit in a trade while momentum dwindles (unless you're sure it will pick up again).

You can look at the various time frames available to you to work out if the price has chances of hitting your take profit or your stop loss. For example, suppose you find that the price has found support on the hourly chart and gone up because it's oversold, and on the four-hour, the momentum shows you signs that the move is almost over. In that case, consider exiting your trade rather than waiting for it to hit your take profit level.

However, if it turns out that the weekly, daily, and four-hour charts are telling you the price will continue to move your way, but the hourly chart claims it won't, then you should definitely ignore the hourly and maintain your higher time frame focus.

This is easier said than done because you might want to take your money and run. However, letting your profits run is how you win in this game — that and cutting your losses short. If you're so nervous about losing that you can't even sleep or look away from your charts, then your lot size and leverage are way too large for that account. You want only to risk money that won't bother you if you lose it.

Keep in mind that momentum is just one of many tools to help you work out the speed of price, and it's not always an indicator of direction. For instance, you should be very suspicious when the price begins to move too hard and too fast.

Ask yourself where it's going, and then go wait for that level before taking a trade or figuring out what you need to do. Momentum can come during stop hunts when the Central Banks seek liquidity to take in the opposite direction. So, whatever you do, never chase trades you didn't plan for. To phrase that better, never chase trades, period. You'll get burned if you try.

Using Candlestick Formations

Candlestick patterns are useful tools, but they're only as effective as the context they appear in. For instance, you wouldn't try to sell triple top in a downtrend (unless you're using higher time frames to pick your short bias). On the other hand, reversal patterns are great on a higher time frame because they can give you massive rewards.

Many trading gurus and books tell you that you can pay attention to candlestick patterns in any time frame they form. Still, the pros who actually trade for a living know that the higher time frames are judge, jury, and executioner. They have a lot more significance than any other time frame out there.

A candlestick pattern that shows up on the weekly chart or daily chart offers you explosive movement worth hundreds of pips over the coming weeks and days. While other newbies are scratching their heads, wondering why the price is rallying or dropping with such ferocity, you'll know it's because there was a clear signal it would do so on one of these time frames. Again, that significantly increases your trading edge.

Also, candlesticks on the daily and weekly time frames offer you very well-defined price levels so that you can look for reactions within a smaller time frame. This is why you should take your time to look at these levels. You might say to yourself, "But then I won't trade every day!" but trading is not like a desk job where you must work nine to five. The best traders know this and never try to force a trade. They just wait for their levels to be hit, and then they execute their plan. Besides, there are so many Forex pairs you could trade, so you should find a good setup or two easily each week that will pay you more than your job or bank ever will. So why rush?

There's a catch with daily and weekly candlesticks, though. They will only give you a general direction to look at, like a recent push to the upside that seems just about ripe for a drop back down. The Forex market requires that you think in terms of probabilities. So, it's not that the price must go down or reverse completely. It might just stall there.

Realize that candlestick patterns don't necessarily give you entry and exit prices. So, trading them requires a lot of faith because your stop will be higher - unless you do the intelligent thing and drop down to a lower time frame after you've got your higher time frame confirmation.

Look for your best setups, and then get in the trade. A daily double top means the price should drop, but it doesn't mean the price will drop right away or drop from that candle's close. It might need to make one last little push to the upside first before it makes its way down.

Chapter Eight: Managing the Trade

Now you're in a trade, and all you have to do is let the Forex gods do their thing and give you some money, right? Well, that's not how it works. You can't just sit by and do nothing like it's a casino, and you've placed your best, and that's it (unless that's actually a crucial part of your strategy, in which case, please ignore me).

For the most part, you will need to keep an eye on your trades because the market is a very dynamic place. New things happen every second.

This doesn't mean you should never take your eyes off the charts, but it does mean you should be ready at a moment's notice to adjust if you get clear evidence from your charts that you should be exiting your trade, taking partials, or trailing your stops to protect what's yours.

How much managing you have to do comes down to the kind of trading you're doing (scalping, swinging, or day trading) as well as the market conditions you're working with (whether trending or ranging).

If your strategy is long to medium term and your stop-loss is wider than other traders, you will likely have a set-and-forget approach to trading. However, it doesn't hurt to stay on top of the market. To prevent prematurely exiting, you should have clear parameters that tell you when you should do something or sit on your hands.

There's really no option for day traders and scalpers but to remain on top of what's going on. They're looking to take smaller pieces of the pie, and things can change a little too fast on the lower time frames, where movement comes with speed and is temporary.

If you have a strategy that only captures the tiny price movements, you will need to be more proactive about protecting your wins and keeping your risk minimal because short-term reversals can take you out of the game. Also, the shorter time frames mean you should plan your exits accordingly.

You can't be held for 450 pips when the idea you framed your trade on is based on the one-minute chart. That right there is how to lose your account 101. You should be gunning for 10 to 50 pips, or an excellent average of 20 because those numbers are more realistic for the lower time frames.

Keep an eye out for news events and price action while you're in a trade. There could be unexpected news that may or may not work out in your favor. For example, if you're in a trade and price suddenly rallies by 100 pips because of an event, don't let those pips get away.

Instead, you can trail your stop, or better yet, close part of your position. Or, if you prefer, you can do both, making sure you don't trail your stop so close to the price that you lose out on even more gains if the price continues in your favor.

You should already have figured out how much money you're willing to lose before you get in a trade. Most newbies only ever think about the money. They don't think about the very real fact that they could lose.

It's why they go and bet the farm and then lose their shirts when things don't go how they wanted them to. So always know what your risk is.

Figure out how much you want to lose on that trade, pinpoint where you want your stop loss to be relative to the spot price, and then use an online risk calculator to help you determine what your lot size should be. Factor in your trading commissions as well if your broker charges you for those.

Whatever you do, your stop loss should only move to secure profits, not allow losses. Some people get so cocky or hopeful, and then they adjust their stop losses as the trade goes against them, sure the price won't take them out (or hoping it doesn't, anyway).

Then just like that, they've taken on an even more significant loss than they were planning for. If it helps you, don't think of yourself as a Forex trader but a risk manager. Your only job is to protect your capital at all costs. Any benefits you accrue from trading are just bonuses.

It doesn't sound fun, I know, but trust me, you will grow your account beyond your imaginations with this mindset. This is why you should only risk what you can lose.

A general rule of thumb is only to risk 2 percent of your account per trade. The trouble with this is that some people follow that rule, but then they open a bajillion positions, and then when things go against them, they lose *a lot.*

So, here's what I'm suggesting to you: Never have more than 2 percent of your account *in total* exposure to the market. In other words, if you're going to risk 2 percent on a trade, then that had better be your only trade until it has played out entirely or until you have secured at least 6 percent in profits before you put on another.

Even better, you can allocate 0.25 percent to each trade. This should be an amount you're okay with losing. If your account is large (which it shouldn't be until you have doubled a small account, at least), then you might want to risk even less per trade.

With 0.25 percent, you can put on 8 trades at any single time. This allows you to diversify your risk and take advantage of other pairs if you're looking at more than one.

Using Alerts

Your charting platform can be set up to send you email alerts or push notifications so that you know when the price is at your level of interest. Just look up how to do that on your trading platform.

For MT4, you might need an E (expert advisor, otherwise, all you'll get are sound and popup alerts. If you can't have sound, some good, free EAs out there can be set up to send you price alerts on your mobile MT4 or as email alerts.

Using alerts is a great way to keep you informed of what the market is doing. It also helps you sit on your hands and not interrupt your trades when you're a set and forget trader. This is because you'll only get an alert if your trade has smashed the take profit level or your stop loss has been hit.

If you can't run your computer all the time, you should consider investing in a VPS. Your charting platform and/or broker should be able to offer you this service, and it's relatively cheap, too.

With the VPS, you can set up your EAs and alerts, and even when your computer isn't online, you'll get alerts about what's going on with your price levels or with your trade. This is a worthwhile investment, especially if you have a day job and can't keep taking time off work to look at the markets.

But, please, don't assume that these alerts will do anything to your trade. You must set the orders or adjust them yourself. All they do is let you know when the specific price you're interested in has been reached.

Has the thought occurred to you that you could set an alert at a price if your trade isn't working out rather than a stop loss? Please don't do this.

The markets can move so fast sometimes that by the time you open up your platform to close the trade, you'd be lucky if you still had any ammo left to take shots at the charts with. Your broker executes your orders, not your price alerts.

Watch Other Markets

There are other markets besides the Forex market, like commodities, bonds, and stocks. Over the long term, they have shown that they correlate with the Forex market. However, they aren't as reliable as predictors of what will happen with currencies in the shorter term.

Still, there are very vital relationships between the other markets and the currency market. After all, these markets need currency to exist. These relationships mainly affect the US Dollar, which is "king," because the US economy is the world's leader. So, you want to see what's happening in other markets so you know if they're confirming your bias and price movement in the Forex markets or if there's some fishy contradiction going on.

Again, you can't trade based on the information you get from these markets in the short term, but you will definitely be ahead of the curve and able to anticipate emerging trends in the coming months and quarters, at least.

US Treasury Yields

This is definitely worth checking in with, as it will show you the general direction that the US interest rates will be headed in. You want to focus on the US ten-year Treasury note yield because this is the one interest rate worth watching.

Also, notice the shorter-term yields like the two-year notes and the three-month Treasury bills. When the yields rise, this is bullish for the dollar and bearish for other currencies. When they fall, it's bearish for the Dollar and bullish for other currencies.

If the yields are bullish, yet the Dollar isn't rising, that means there are other things at play suppressing the Dollar, and bullish traders need to keep their eyes wide open. If the yields drop and the dollar drops along with it, you should see lower interest rates.

You must watch the bond yield's price action, as it can show you different scenarios going on in the market. If it moves in alignment with the interest rate expectations because of Fed comments or other events, chances are you will know the direction of the US dollar. If it's on account of uncertainty in the market, or anything else like Europe's debt concerns, then you might see the Dollar affected positively. The more dramatic the change in the yields, the louder the message from the bond market. If you see that the yield has changed over 1 percent, this should make you sit up.

Safe Havens

Silver and gold are precious metals used to hedge against inflation. When the faith in the US economy goes down, people flock to these metals because they're real, physical, finite, and valuable, unlike the US Dollar, which the Fed prints and prints ad infinitum (as a government-sanctioned scam called ***quantitative easing).***

So, it's no surprise that lately, silver and gold have seen a lot more demand as alternatives to the Almighty Dollar. The Euro also has its own fair share of struggles. For this reason, gold and silver will move in the opposite direction to the Dollar. This is called ***inverse correlation.***

Trying to work out any short-term correlation is a really tricky thing to do. Silver and gold, for all their worth, aren't as liquid as the Dollar. Also, the only reason they are in high demand is because of what happens with currencies.

So, look for evidence that the US dollar is plummeting or rising. You can tell by looking at the price of these precious metals. If the Dollar is flying, then you know the metals are falling (or at least, they should be), and that's a good thing because it means you can trust the gains the Dollar is making. However, if the Dollar is rallying, and gold is still holding a steady price or even rallying right along with the Greenback, then that means you should be very suspicious of the Dollar's strength.

Black Gold

Let's talk about oil. This black, liquid gold is just like real gold, silver, and other commodities, in that it is inversely correlated with the US Dollar over the long term. In other words, if oil is up, then the Dollar is down, and if oil is down, then the Dollar is up.

However, just like with precious metals, you have to beware of the correlations in the short term, as they aren't reliable. Oil, in particular, is susceptible to demand and supply shocks that only affect it and nothing else.

Also, there's an asymmetric bias to its relationship with the US Dollar, which means that oil will have strength on a falling Dollar but may not necessarily grow weak just because the Dollar is rising, all things being equal.

Keep an eye out for the developments in price so that you have an idea of what might happen with the interest rates and the economic growth. When oil prices are higher, there are usually rising inflation pressures which can subsequently cause interest rates to go higher.

Also, higher oil prices can reduce the economy's growth as personal consumption of this black gold goes down. Between both, the impact oil has on economic growth matters more on account of how quickly consumers react to oil price fluctuations.

However, interest rate changes will need more time. The rapid growth of emerging markets has led to a worldwide demand for this liquid, so oil is starting to serve as a tool to measure global economic growth.

Stocks

Over the long term, and in particular the last decade, there hasn't been much correlation between currencies and the stock market. Still, from 2008 to 2009, when the Great Financial Crisis happened, there's been more correlation between Forex and stocks, particularly when it comes to the US Dollar. The connection is a risk-on/risk-off one, in that stocks are assets considered risk-seeking, and the Dollar is a safe-haven asset.

Put simply, if you're doing well, you don't mind spending some dollars on stocks or having your *risk on* the market. If you think stocks are terrible right now and you're broke anyway, you'd rather liquidate them and have your Dollars or *risk-off.*

Investors will purchase Dollars to buy US Treasury debt, which is the perfect safe harbor. Recently, here's how this has played out: When the market is bullish, investors heartily open their arms to the risk and spend their Dollars on stocks. This causes a drop in the demand for Dollars, which causes the Dollar to lose strength. When everything goes south, the investors dump their stocks and rush right back to the safe, loving arms of the Greenback and the US Treasuries.

As long as financial issues plague the global economy, this relationship remains relatively fixed. However, suppose there are financial and economic conditions that improve things so that things are almost normal. In that case, chances are Forex and stocks will go back to having lower correlations.

Tweaking Your Trade Plan with Time

Like most traders, once you're in a position, you're aware of every pip that moves for you and against you - if your eyes are on the screen, of course. So, with each little movement in your floating profits and losses, you feel all kinds of emotions, from ecstasy to grief. There's nothing unusual about this, especially initially, since what matters the most in your eyes is the profit and loss balance.

What's weirdly overlooked by traders for some reason is the idea of time. The price of an asset remains where it is for a long while, or it just keeps bouncing about in a range, but time relentlessly marches on.

Submitting yourself to time is a skill you need to learn as a trader. You know what's going on with the price right now. The only thing that needs to be answered is where will the market head next? When you think about it, it all comes down to time. It's easy to look at a chart and figure out possible levels price will head to (at least, once you've studied the charts for long enough), but then everyone seems to forget that time is a factor.

When back testing strategies or going over past candles, it's easy to forget that each candlestick represents price action **over a time frame**. So, ask yourself, can you be patient? Can you submit to time and sit on your hands unless and until you're supposed to act?

As time passes, things happen on the charts. You have daily fixings and options expiring, among other things. These are when you can expect a rush of activity, though this doesn't always play out that way. As time passes, you also get closer to scheduled data and news events.

The market expectations are priced in the days and hours **before** that news release. When the time draws close, the market goes quiet. There isn't much speculation because everyone is waiting to react to whatever happens. Then, just before the figures are released, things get erratic with the price as traders liquidate positions or pile in their OCO orders to capitalize on whatever happens next. The price chops around but never goes anywhere, really. These things happen because of the news event and time as well.

Objectively speaking, as time passes on, it can add more importance to the movements of the price that have taken place already. It can also take away the significance of price. As a result, many trading signals are generated. For example, say the price fails to close below a trend line support on an hourly chart. This could indicate that the break was a false one and that price really wants to head back up and beyond old highs.

However, if the break happened by 9:04, you won't know about it until the hourly candle closes 56 minutes later. More signals pop up from the longer time frames, like a daily candle close above a higher time frame trend line or an old daily swing high. For this reason, you need to be aware of what's happening with the price so that you can make any necessary adjustments to your trade.

Say you're taking trades using trend lines. First, you must know that the price levels you get from your trend lines will change depending on its slope or angle to your chart's horizontal axis. The steeper this slope is, the more the change will be to the significant price level with time. Conversely, the shallower the slope of the trend line, the less critical the price will be when it touches it, so you might want to avoid trading that.

With your charting platform, you can work out almost accurately where price will get to in the future for your trendline to remain valid support or resistance. To do this, slide your cursor along the line, then look at the time it lines up at the bottom of your chart. Are you starting to understand the many ways in which time matters in Forex?

This same idea applies to longer-term charts, but the shifts in price are far less dramatic, which means a trend line on an hourly chart may adjust its levels every 12 hours or 6 hours by 10 or 15 pips, while the daily charts will have their levels shift by 10 to 30 pips over some days. The rules aren't set in stone on this. It all comes down to the angle of the trend line in question.

Regardless of the time frame you plan your trades on, you want to keep the shifting trend line levels in mind, especially if you use them for trading. This also means you will need to adjust your orders.

For short-term positions and overnight ones, you should think about where the trend line resistance or support will be in the next 6 hours, or 12 hours at the most, while your position remains active, but you can't monitor your charts. It might help to use a trailing stop.

For your limit entries, if they are based on a trend line's slope, you will have to adjust your order every now and then so that it still works out in line with the changes in price relative to the trend line. If you don't do this, you may miss a trade entry when the price hits the trend line or get triggered too late at a lousy price.

When trading breakouts, major trend lines that seem to be so far away in one week might suddenly be really close by the next week or two. This means your outlook on the market should adjust accordingly. Or the market may be homing in on a particular low or high as the trigger for a breakout when your sloping trend line at that level is the main point for the momentous move.

New Events, New Adjustments

As you work on your trading plan, you should really make a habit of looking at the news calendar to see the events that line up for the week ahead. It bears repeating because you do not want to be caught unawares when the Central Banks push the price to places that hurt you.

Always check for the scheduled events to come, even in a trade. If you follow this top religiously, you will reduce the odds of your trades being blown out of the water by predictable and expected events - expected by everyone and their grandmother but you.

Keeping an eye on news events will also make it possible for you to forecast where the price wants to go and where there should be strong reactions for you to take advantage of. Take the time to look at the news if you haven't been doing so since you began your trading journey.

Look at what happens to the price from a higher time frame perspective with each high-impact news release. Also, study the levels created over the days leading up to the news event on a lower time frame. Remember how I mentioned that news excites the market for a bit, but then the market must get back in line with the trend? You'll start to see how this plays out often, and with the intel you get, you will know precisely how to trade the move that comes after the news, when things have settled down at last.

Tightening Your Stop Loss Order

You must be aggressive about protecting your capital. You're no ordinary trader. You're a risk manager, so managing risk should be the chief goal. Imagine you've sat in a trade for days, and it's been going your way for about 150 pips, but you didn't take some profits, and you didn't bother to move your stop loss to break even either.

Then suddenly, the price comes right back down and not only smacks you out of the trade but takes your money too. How would that feel? Not very good, I imagine.

Or here's another scenario (it's never going to happen, but just roll with it): Your boss asks you to put in overtime at work. You agree to it, and he has said he'll pay you extra on top of your usual daily take home, on the condition that you take off at precisely 6 PM.

If you don't leave by 6 PM, not only will he not pay you the extra money, he'll also make sure you don't even get a dime. So why would you stick around past 6

PM? If anything, you will make sure you're out by 5:58 PM and tell him he can deduct whatever's worth those 2 minutes left from your pay.

Or imagine some wealthy philanthropist is throwing money around and making a game of it. You can take as much money as you can catch and put it into a little basket. You may empty out this basket wherever you want to keep your money safe and keep catching more as it falls from the sky. Also, of course, there's a time limit for this.

What would you think if you saw someone with a full basket, trying to catch more money but losing precious Dollar bills because what's in the basket keeps pouring out? Wouldn't the smart thing be to secure what you've got so that you can have room for more?

These analogies may sound silly, but it's the exact same thing many new traders do when they're in a trade. They want to get a perfect score. They want to get out at precisely 50 pips. "What do you mean get out at 499 points? Are you nuts?" So, the price gets to their take profit, but the broker's spread isn't wide enough to hit it.

Then they sit there and give back everything they gained to the markets and pay the price of greed by having their stop loss hit. Does this sound familiar? We've all been there. This is why you need strict rules for securing your trades.

First, you must work out the price levels you want to take your profits at, whether in full or partially. You should also know how many pips you want the trade to move before making the trade risk-free by moving your stop loss to break even, accounting for commissions and the spreads.

Ideally, the best way to secure your trades is by using price action. When the price hits an old low if you're selling (or an old high if you're buying), take some money off the table.

You could also move your stop to break even after the price has created a new swing low above your buy trade or a new swing high below your sell trade. This way, you won't get knocked out on the inevitable retracement before the rally or the drop.

You can use a moving average to slide your stop loss along as the price goes your way. This same practice can work with trend lines as well. For example, you can look at Fibonacci levels, wait to see them broken, and then move your stop loss to the broken level.

When the support and resistance points you use have been exceeded by price, this means the market is willing to move the price even higher or lower in your trade direction, so you can move your stop loss close to the damaged areas, leaving enough room for the spread, so you're not taken out.

Keep in mind that the more aggressively you adjust your stops, the more likely it is that you'll miss out on good moves if the direction is right, and the price comes back for your stops in a pullback. If you like, you can use a trailing stop loss and no take profit if you're sure that the price will move your way considerably.

Chapter Nine: Risk, Money, and Emotional Management

You may be tempted to skip this one, but for the sake of your sanity, your account balance, everything, and everyone you hold dear, there is no good reason to. This chapter will make you cringe, but don't you dare put this book down. I promise you will be glad you didn't.

The Forex industry is full of scammers. They prey on newbies because they know that it's easy to impress them with affluent lifestyles and screenshots of winning trades. They know that new traders aren't thinking about risk to reward ratios, money management skills, or losses.

This is why they're able to sucker people in and rip them off with their fake signals, fake MyFXbook records, fake screenshots, fake signal services, manipulated trades, and fake dollar bills splayed on their borrowed MacBook's in rented AirBnB's that they claim they own. Read this chapter, and you won't be one of the sheep they lead to the slaughter.

Hey Loser

Most new traders think that the way to making their bread and butter (and then some) is to have the highest leverage a broker could offer, the highest lot sizes their accounts can take on a single trade, and the highest account balance possible.

So, they start off risking more money they can lose, and they eventually blow their accounts. People have lost their homes and families because of this unrealistic view of the markets. There's no need to be one of them.

First things first, how much money do you want to put into your very first trading account? Before you answer that, let me tell you this: ***You're going to lose it.*** Well, that's not a very nice thing to say, right? Did you choose to read this book because you want to be told costly lies or because you want to make money? I assume it's the latter. Of course, you're going to make money, but first things first, you need to **understand** and **accept** that you're going to lose money.

To put things in better perspective: Every trader who puts trade on is a losing trader. When your order goes live, you're immediately in the red until the price goes your way. Also, every newbie trader will lose money. It's part of the learning process. Just think of it as the cost of learning to make more money than you've ever dreamed by just clicking a red button or a blue one.

Here's something else you need to know: ***You want to lose money.*** I know that sounds confusing, but listen, you want to lose money now, and fast. The sooner you do, the more immune you become to the idea of losing money, and the faster you can move your attention away from your cash and pips to **percentages.**

If you start off as a winning trader right off the bat, you're going to get cocky and arrogant, and sooner or later, the market will humble you. Unfortunately, that "humbling" could be very expensive, so it's better to have that experience now and at a lower price.

So, let's get back to the question, how much money will you put in your first trading account? $100,000? Make it $10,000. If it's $10,000, make it $1,000. If it's $1,000, make it $100.

I know you probably think a tenth of your original amount is too small to make anything significant, but this isn't about making money right now. It's about managing your emotions around money so that you can make money consistently.

90 percent of traders lose money, and it's not because they have terrible strategies. It's not because their broker keeps hitting their stops (although some brokers do that). It's not because they don't work at Wallstreet.

So, what's the real reason? It's because they don't have the first clue about managing their emotions around money. Sure, they have all the fancy indicators and EAs with the bells and whistles, but not a clue how important it is to manage your risk, your money, and the person you see in the mirror every morning. I'll prove it to you.

Risk Reward Ratios

Say you have a strategy that gives you a win rate of 30 percent (which is the lowest win rate you should have, otherwise you really need to finetune your system, or you won't make any money). This means for every 10 trades you take, you lose 7, and you win 3. Let's assume that you risk 1 percent of your account balance, and you're trading with $100. I know it's not a sexy figure, but that's the point. You must wean your mind off of money for now.

If your trade setups give you three times your risk each time (a 1:3 risk to reward ratio), let's work out the math. You lose $7 for every ten trades you take, **but** you make $9 on your profitable trades. This means you're up to $2.

With a risk-reward ratio of 1:5, you may lose $7 for every ten trades you take, but your winning trades are $5 each, which come up to $15, so you're not positive by $8.

If your win rate is only 20 percent, and your risk-reward is 1:5, you lose $8, but you make $2 because your gross profit is $10. Are you starting to get the picture? Everyone's always looking for the Holy Grail of trading strategies. They want hundreds of thousands of pips and a 200 percent win rate. I'll tell you this for free: ***It doesn't exist***. Actually, there is a holy grail, but I'll share that with you at the end of the book.

The point of this is simple: You always want to make sure your risk-reward ratio is **at least** 1:3. Some people say 1:2 or 1:1. I say keep it 1:3, even if you're starting out. This is also why you should reduce your trading balance by a tenth, so you're not too bothered by your losses.

Don't get me wrong, you'll hate losing, but you won't want to jump off a cliff because you just lost a million-dollar loan, either. In this book, you have so many strategies you can use to get 1:3 setups. It's not impossible for you.

If you trade higher time frame setups with lower time frame entries, a 1:10 risk-reward ratio is possible. But, again, it all comes down to your ability to be patient. If you aren't, don't worry. The market teaches all of us to be patient, assuming you don't quit just because of a few blown accounts, and you continue to study what works and discard what doesn't.

Percentages, Not Pips, Not Dollars

If someone said, "Hey, I make 3 percent every week," most new traders would follow that up with the question, "Okay, but how much do you make, though?" This focus on dollar figures and the number of pips leads to greed and terrible trading decisions. Yes, the goal is to make money, but you won't do that obsessing over how much you pulled in.

What you need to understand is that 3% a week is fantastic. Even three percent a month is excellent. Why? Three percent could be three percent of $1,000,000, which is $30,000. ***Not a lousy trading month at all.*** Focusing on Dollar signs is what leads to taking profits too early.

As I've demonstrated, this is a terrible thing to do because it makes it more likely that you will blow your account when the losing streak comes: And it comes for everyone, even the pros. If it didn't, no one would bother talking about defining risk and managing money properly.

Money Management

Risk management is about working out your risk and taking steps to reduce it, while money management is about reducing your losses and maximizing your wins.

Can't lose it? Don't trade it. We've already discussed rule number one: you should only trade what you can afford to lose. Not only should you reduce the capital you start off with by a tenth, but you should also make sure that every month, you have a fixed percentage of losses you're willing to take, and after that, you will close your platform and walk away till the next month. Don't trade with money that you need to survive on either because that will do your head in when you lose.

Don't know your risk per trade? Don't take the trade. Next, work out your allowed risk for each trade.

Some people have a fixed sum of money in their heads. That can work, too, as long as you keep the reward three times that amount, and you're not going overboard with the trading. For example, you could decide when you're more profitable to risk $50 for every $5,000 you have. If you take only ten trades a day, then you know you won't risk more than $500 that day.

The trouble with risking fixed amounts is you don't account for the wins or losses you make. You could have a winning streak and grow your account exponentially, or you could have a losing streak and lose by a whole lot.

Others risk a fixed percentage of their account balance. So, a $10,000 account means you will only risk $200 on any given trade if your risk per trade is 2 percent. The good thing about this method is that your risk matches your account balance.

When you're on a winning streak, your account grows accordingly, and so does the amount of money you can risk on subsequent trades. Conversely, when you lose, your risk per trade will reduce along with your balance, meaning it might take you a while to make your money back *if you don't have a sound higher time frame strategy.*

Make your risk-reward ratio work for you. You already know about the risk to reward ratios—1:3 only. If a trade setup doesn't give you at least three times what you're risking, let it go. The market will generously give you a better setup another time.

Leverage is your friend. And your enemy. I've addressed this at the start of the book in that it allows you to take on larger positions than your account can handle. So, if you have a 1:200 leverage on a #500 account, you can open up a position worth $100,000.

Sounds incredible, but it is a double-edged sword you might fall on if you haven't learned to be disciplined or don't follow your trading rules. You could make more, but you could also lose more. So just because a broker offers you 1:1000 leverage doesn't mean you should take it.

Withdraw your profit. You earned it. Finally, you should withdraw your earnings when you make them. Most traders starting out don't withdraw their profits as often as they should. So, when you finally make a good amount on your trades, withdraw it and spend it on something meaningful. This will show you that you can make a living trading Forex and that you, in fact, just did that. It also keeps the fire fresh within you to dance with the markets, week after week.

Set up your trading rules where you can see them. You could write:

- I won't risk more than 2% of my total account balance at any given time in the market.

- I will only take trades with a 1:3 risk-reward ratio or more.
- I will stop trading for the week if I lose 5% of my account.

You can adjust that list accordingly.

Reduce your risk after a losing trade. For example, if you risked 2 percent, cut it down to 1 on the next trade. If you lose that one again, cut it down to .5 percent. If you lose that one, cut it down to .25 percent and continue to trade that risk until your account is back up to where it was before you lost 1 percent, then take it back up to .5%.

If you're taking the higher time frame trades I've talked about repeatedly, you will find this very beneficial. Also, when you trade like this, your equity curve looks smooth and beautiful, and you can get people to invest with you (when you are accredited to trade on other's behalf, of course).

Cut your risk in half after a string of winners. Ideally, cut them in half if you have five winners in a row. This keeps your emotions in check so you don't get a big head and go higher when you should trade smaller. Besides, the more your account balance grows, the less risk you need to take on to make the same significant amounts you did in the past. Also, you protect yourself against a losing streak this way and keep that equity curve looking healthy.

Mindset

You must make peace with losing. The way to do that is to understand that one bad trade doesn't make you a bad trader. You could be right about the direction but wrong about that trade. Other times, the trade was right, but the market pulled one of its stunts. It happens. Please don't beat yourself up when you have losing trades or blow your accounts. With time, patience, and practice, you will begin to see some consistency in your trading.

When you feel like risking more than you should, remind yourself that the name of the game is longevity. You want to make sure, even if you have a string of losers when the market starts to do as you expect again and gives you the best setups, you have money to trade them. What's the point in blowing it all on one trade?

Think about the magic of compound interest, and let it work in your favor. You make money in Forex not by risking everything you have but by taking quality setups that continue to pay you. Consider hunting for trades daily or weekly, and you'll start to see why you shouldn't bother with lower time frames (other than to get tighter entries and stop losses).

Stop and check in with how you feel before you open up the charts. Our emotions affect us more than we know. If you don't feel great that day, don't trade. If not, you'll lose money and wish you had just stayed away.

Review your trades. Especially the losers. You learn more from your losses than your wins. So don't be afraid to analyze failed trades. This is how you become a better trader.

Think long-term. Yes, it would be lovely to have that Lambo and "flex on your haters," but that shouldn't be your goal. Instead, focus on learning first, and then you will earn for sure.

Meditate. I can't stress this enough. You only need ten to fifteen minutes each day to see results. You will notice you trade with a calmer approach, not jumping willy-nilly at every pip that moves.

Spend as much time as you can with your charts. A strange thing happens the more you look at the charts. You start to see things that you realize in the back of your mind you always knew were there, but now they're a lot clearer to you. This is how you develop that trader's intuition the pros have.

Stay off trading forums. Seriously, if you can just choose one strategy and learn the ins and outs of it, it will pay you. Trading forums can be incredibly toxic sometimes, full of failed traders looking to tell you it can't be done, or your strategy sucks. Some traders share setups completely against your bias, and you change your mind about your trade only to learn you were right. Leave the forums and focus on yourself.

Get a mentor. Find someone who knows the ropes, someone who actually makes withdrawals and can prove it. Shadow them, learn from them, and you will see exponential growth.

Chapter Ten: Mistakes Forex Traders Make

There are so many mistakes that Forex traders make coming into the industry. It's sad because it's so easy for anyone to get started with trading, as long as they have the internet, a laptop, and a few dollars to burn. If only it were as easy to take money out of the markets as it is to put it in. Before you get into trading, here are things you should be on the lookout for:

Mistake #1: Revenge trading. You enter a trade, and it loses. So rather than waiting for another setup, you force the trade, and it takes you out again. Now you're Hulk-smash mad!

So, you go in with max lots because how dare your broker take your money from you? "How dare the markets treat me like crap? Give me back my money!" you cry inside you. Then you lose it all with just a few measly pips of movement.

What happened? Your emotions. We're all emotional. Even the best of traders feel things. So, add this to your rules. When I take a losing trade, I will walk away and go do something else for a few hours before I come back to evaluate what went wrong or take another trade.

Mistake #2: Not using a stop loss. This is an excellent way to lose your money. You must make sure every trade has a set stop loss. If you're worried about it getting hit, set it at a previous swing. Don't try to cheat the markets by making it tighter than it should be. Give yourself more room and adjust your trade size accordingly. You don't need to be perfect. You only need to make bank.

Mistake #3: Adding to your losers. When you have a losing position, don't add to your trade. You don't know if the market will go your way. You can't say for sure. Remember, it's all probability. I'll quote this again, "The markets can stay irrational longer than you can remain solvent." Allow the trade to play out. If it hits your stop loss, that would be a lot better than losing more than you should have.

Mistake #4: Trading every day. Just because the markets are open 24/5 doesn't mean you have to be in trade the whole time. Sometimes the best setups come in the middle of the week. So don't be in a hurry to trade. Allow the market to show you its plans for the week on Sunday and Monday, and then you can stalk your setups after.

Mistake #5: Cutting profits short. This happens when you've taken a loss or more, and you badly want to make up for it. So rather than allow the trade to go where you expect it to, you take a few measly pips to balance out your account. When you do this, you limit yourself, and you'll really feel the heat when more losers come.

Mistake #6: Using Martingale. Unless you have Bezos fat pockets or Elon-Esque bank accounts, please stay away from this terrible strategy. Martingale's money management method involves doubling up on your losses when you take the next trade. For example, say you lose $1.

Then you risk $2. If you win, that should give you $6 with a 1:3 win reward ratio, which puts your account in a profit of $5 net. However, what happens when you have a string of losers (which statistics prove occurs to the best of traders too)? You don't want to go down that road.

Mistake #6: Trading the news. It doesn't matter how many times you traded the news successfully on your demo account. Don't do it. Demo market conditions are different from live markets. The increased volatility during news events makes it almost impossible for your broker to fill you in at the prices you want, and the spreads will destroy your account.

Mistake#7: Trading with the wrong broker. Do your homework before you settle on a brokerage firm. Some of them are outright scams. You can trade, but once it's time to withdraw, you won't be able to. So only choose brokers that are accredited and regulated by national and international bodies.

Mistake #8: Trading too many correlated pairs at the same time. Diversification is an excellent strategy to reduce your risk, but it's not diversifying when you trade USD/JPY, EUR/USD, USD/CAD, and USD/ZAR simultaneously. What's wrong with this picture? You have Dollars everywhere, and not in a good way.

If some news happens, or there's a sudden movement in price against you, you could lose way more than you should have. On the other hand, if you notice the exact same setup happening across specific pairs all the time, those pairs are correlated.

So just pick the best one. You can also check online to learn more about which pairs correlate with each other the most, whether positively or inversely.

Mistake #9: Trading economic data. The news says the Dollar is dropping or will drop. You open up your chart, and you see a different story, but you heard it on the news, so they must know what they're saying, and you go short on it. Then you lose. The talking heads don't know what they're talking about, for the most part.

Observe what they say and what the charts say for a while, and you'll see that too. If they seem knowledgeable, it's only because their statements always happen...***eventually***. Obviously, the price will go down, and the price will go up. The real questions are when and at what price. They don't know that. Also, long-term "funny mentals" don't matter when you're a day trader.

News is heavily manipulated. If you know what to look for in the charts, you will find that the levels were already priced in for a particular event involving towers and planes, and a specific global flu, **before** those events happened. This sounds like a conspiracy theory, but it's not *if you know what to look for.* I could easily write a whole book on that topic to show you how, time and time again, the charts show that these events were expected.

The silver flash crash, the black swan event, and any other event give the market maker the excuse to take the price they want to go. The easiest way to manipulate the masses of newbie traders is to tell them they should pay attention to the news.

A perfect example is Elon Musk shilling Bitcoin. When everyone listened, the price dropped. Meanwhile, he had acquired a fair bit before he made that infamous tweet. As a rule, "Be fearful when they're greedy and greedy when they're fearful."

Mistake #10: Paying for scam signals and account management. Your broker might have the option to manage your account for you. That's fine. However, if you see some random accounts or comments on YouTube or any other social media platform talking about how Mr. Sean Connery and Miss Betty White traded for them and made them a bunckojillian dollars, run the other way.

Stay away from Telegram signals too. Most of them will offer you free signals that steal from other legit traders (at best, so you make money) or which are totally made up (at worst, so you lose money) and then ask you to join their paid service. You send them some money, and then they block you. Also, don't pay for any course without checking out the reviews. A lot of these "trading gurus" are demo ballers and marketers. You can get some excellent information for free on YouTube.

Mistake #11: Believing in screenshots. This one is a doozy, but you can actually set up your Forex charts on MT4 to look like you took an actual trade and caught it right at the bottom. There's also an app that can do this with your phone. This is why I say don't fall for the screenshots.

Don't fall for the fake dollar bills either, or traders who claim to live "that FX lifestyle," making "fousands and fousands of dollars." (If you ask traders who have been in the business a long while, they know who that is.)

If they can show you their withdrawals, then you can believe them. So instead of following what is called "trader porn" in the industry, focus on your charts and getting better.

Now you know the most common mistakes Forex traders, new and old, make. So, the question is, what are the habits of profitable traders who consistently pull in money ***and keep it?*** If you want to become a successful trader yourself, then start your Forex journey living and trading by these rules.

Tip #1: Never trade without a plan. If you don't have a trading plan, you won't last very long in the game. You must have a plan for every trade you take. You might be able to wing it successfully in the short term, but one day, your wings won't work, and you'll go down hard.

You want to have a plan for each position, lot sizes, entries, stop losses, take profits, exits, and so on. You can be flexible about your take profits if you have a good reason to anticipate more movement (or expect the trade won't play out anymore), but don't use your stop loss to do the moonwalk.

Tip #2: Be flexible. We already know the only thing you need to be rigid with is your stop. However, don't marry your positions. Don't get so emotionally attached that you don't get out even when it's undeniable that you should. Be quick to abandon a very obvious loser, and you will save more capital to take advantage of a better setup in the future.

Tip #3: Always get screen time. So, you took a taekwondo class ten years ago, and you feel you can beat the reigning champ? Well, I can tell you for sure you'd make a great comedian. You want to keep your skills sharp, and this means looking at your charts. Go through past data for your setups. Remind yourself what works for you and why and be on the lookout for how you can optimize your strategy.

Tip #4: Know that the trend is your friend…until it ends. Following the trend will give you great success in trading, all else being equal. Having said that, when you see obvious signs that you should no longer be in that position but looking the other way, get out. This ties back into staying flexible.

Tip #5: Jealously guard your profits. The market has been giving setups since its inception and always will. You making money from it with every setup, however, isn't guaranteed. So, while you may have a plan for unloading all your positions at your take profit level, make sure you're banking pips along the way. This will also help you psychologically. You should get paid for your time and analysis, at least.

Tip #6: Use a stop loss. If you refuse to use one, your broker will generously help you set one. It's called a margin call, AKA no more money left to trade.

Tip #7: Keep your eye on other markets. Currencies don't exist in a bubble. As mentioned before, pay attention to bond yields, and watch what they do. Then, on your own time, research what markets tend to affect the currencies you trade the most.

Tip #8: Trust your gut. When you put in the work, your subconscious mind picks up on many details that your eyes and brain might be missing. Sometimes you'll be in a trade, and there's absolutely no reason for you to exit or take partials, but then you get the sense that you should. Right when you do, price travels back the other way and would have taken you out and made you pay 1 percent. Trading involves intuition as well, you see. So, each day, make a point to check in with your gut about major decisions, not just in trading but in your life as well. With time, you will have an uncanny knack for knowing when to get in and get out or stay out of the markets.

Conclusion

We've come to the end of this book at last. You now know basic Forex terms and have an idea of what strategies you can trade. You know why you need to figure out the kind of trader you are so that you can capitalize on your strengths in the market. You know why you should pay attention to the charts and what news can and cannot do for you.

So, what happens next? Well, that is entirely up to you, dear reader. I've given you my complete arsenal. I've shared what the trading gurus who want to bleed you dry are hiding from you.

The successful trader is disciplined with their trades and emotions. They know that using indicators only is a deadly trap. They know the importance of staying sharp, following the price closely, looking at it from the macro level. They know that they don't have to take every setup and that they only need a few trades to make significant changes in their accounts.

You have just learned all you need to become one of them. I promised you that I would tell you what the Holy Grail is, and I meant it. Go look in the mirror. There, staring back at you is everything you'll ever need to become a professional Forex trader. The best indicator you could ever have is in between your ears. Use it.

May the pips be with you.

References

Bishop, Paul, and Don Dixon. 1994. Foreign exchange handbook. New York: McGraw-Hill.

Fenton-O'Creevy, Mark, Nigel Nicholson, Emma Soane, and Paul Willman. 2005. Traders: Risks, decisions, and management in financial markets. Oxford University Press.

Goodwin, Jason. 2003. Greenback. New York: Henry Holt.

Harris, Larry. 2003. Trading and exchanges: Market microstructure for practitioners. New York: Oxford University Press.

Harris, Sunny J. 1996. Trading 101. New York: John Wiley & Sons.

J Atkin. 2005. The Foreign Exchange Market of London: Development Since 1900 Psychology Press.

Kleinfield, Sonny. 1983. The traders. New York: Holt, Rinehart, and Winston.

P Mathias, S Pollard. 1989. The Cambridge Economic History of Europe: The industrial economies: the development of economic and social policies Cambridge University Press.

Reinfeld, Fred. 1957. The story of paper money. New York: Sterling Publishing Company.

S Homer, Richard E Sylla. 2005. A History of Interest Rates. John Wiley & Sons.

www.ingramcontent.com/pod-product-compliance
Ingram Content Group UK Ltd.
Pitfield, Milton Keynes, MK11 3LW, UK
UKHW021310180426
11947UKWH00015B/1144